PETER M. DOUBILET, MD, PhD   CAROL B. BENSON, MD   ROANNE WEISMAN

YOUR DEVELOPING BABY

CONCEPTION TO BIRTH

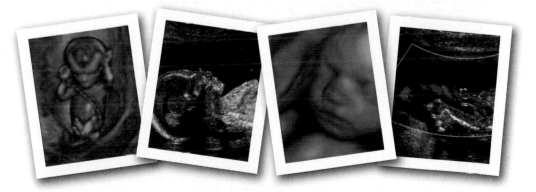

New York   Chicago   San Francisco   Lisbon   London   Madrid   Mexico City
Milan   New Delhi   San Juan   Seoul   Singapore   Sydney   Toronto

Library of Congress Cataloging-in-Publication Data

Doubilet, Peter M.
    Your developing baby, conception to birth : witnessing the miraculous 9-month journey / by Peter M. Doubilet, Carol B. Benson, Roanne Weisman.
        p.   cm.
     ISBN-13: 978-0-07-148871-6 (alk. paper)
     ISBN-10: 0-07-148871-5 (alk. paper)
     1. Embryology, Human—Popular works.   I. Benson, Carol B.   II. Weisman, Roanne, 1952–   III. Title.

QM603.D68 2008
612.6'4—dc22   2007035278

1 2 3 4 5 6 7 8 9 0   SDB/SDB   0 9 8

ISBN 978-0-07-148871-6
MHID   0-07-148871-5

The ultrasound images on pages 70, 113 (A), 114 (H), 131 (bottom), 132, 140, 154, 157, and 170 are reprinted with permission from Doubilet PM, Benson CB. *Atlas of Ultrasound in Obstetrics and Gynecology*. Philadelphia: Lippincott, Williams, and Wilkins, 2003. The ultrasound image on page 33 is reprinted with permission from Benson CB, Doubilet PM. Fetal measurements, normal and abnormal fetal growth. In Rumack C, Charbonneau W, Wilson S, eds. *Diagnostic Ultrasound*, 3rd ed. St. Louis: Yearbook Medical Publishers, 2005, pp. 1493–1512. The ultrasound images on pages 115 and 171 are reprinted with permission from Benson CB. Stuck twin and incompetent cervix or preterm cervical dilation. In Hertzberg B, Cohen H. *Ultrasound III*. Reston, VA: American College of Radiology, 2006. The ultrasound images on pages 10 (A) and 52 (C) are reprinted with permission from Bluth EI, Benson CB, Ralls PW, Siegel MJ (eds.). *Ultrasound: A Practical Approach to Clinical Problems*, 2nd ed. New York: Thieme Medical and Scientific Publishers, 2008.

McGraw-Hill books are available at special quantity discounts to use as premiums and sales promotions or for use in corporate training programs. To contact a representative, please visit the Contact Us pages at www.mhprofessional.com.

This book is printed on acid-free paper.

YOUR
DEVELOPING
BABY
CONCEPTION
TO BIRTH

Contents

Preface   vii

Acknowledgments   xiii

 The Miraculous Journey to a New Life

1   Marvelous Milestones: A Pregnancy Preview   3

2   Preparing for Pregnancy: The Body Gets Ready   17

 The Journey Begins: First Trimester

3   The Pulse of a New Heart: Early First Trimester   29

4   From Structure to Function: Late First Trimester   41

Part 3   **The Growing Baby: Second and Third Trimesters**

5   Don't I Know You? The Face and Head   51

6   A Hub of Activity: Baby's Body   61

7   Shake It Baby! Arms, Legs, and Movement   77

8   Telling the Girls from the Boys: Sexual Organs   87

9   Size Matters: The Baby's Vital Statistics   93

Multiple Pregnancies: Twins, Triplets, and Beyond

10   Double Delight: Twins   107

11   Triplets and More:
Higher-Order Multiple Pregnancies   119

Part 5   **Healthy Mother, Healthy Baby**

12   Baby's Caretakers:
Placenta, Cord, Amniotic Fluid   125

13   Tests for the Baby's Health:
Amniocentesis and Others   137

14   Preventing Problems:
Knowledge Is Power   147

Part 6   **The Main Event: Labor and Birth**

15   A New Life Begins   165

Appendix   179

Index   185

Preface

You may have picked up this book because you or someone you know is embarking on the momentous nine-month journey of pregnancy and you are curious about the miraculous hidden world inside the womb—a world that has become fully visible only recently. After generations of being limited to wondering and imagining, we now have the technology to peer inside the uterus and actually watch the development of a new human being from a tiny group of cells to a fully developed baby, ready to emerge from the mother's body to greet the world.

Through ultrasound images, not only can we see the developing heart, lungs, and other internal organs, we can—thanks to new three-dimensional (3D) ultrasound techniques—see the baby's face and limbs. We can even capture movements of the unborn baby on video. Doctors use these images and videos to check for problems that may arise during pregnancy and to help guide the care of pregnant women. But for parents-to-be, one of the exciting aspects of this technology is the opportunity to start to get to know their baby before the big arrival day. All images in this book were obtained as part of diagnostic medical ultrasounds, performed to give the doctor information about the developing baby and the progress of the pregnancy.

How does ultrasound see the developing life inside a mother's body? Ultrasound imaging, also called *ultrasound scanning* or *sonography*, uses high-frequency sound waves (at a pitch higher than humans can hear) to create images of structures such as organs or blood vessels inside the human body. The process is similar to the sonar used by bats, ships at sea, and anglers with fish detectors. As the sound wave passes through the body, echoes are produced and bounce back, giving information about how far away an object is, how large it is, its shape, and its consistency. A computer then "translates" this information into the ultrasound images—also called *sonograms*—that parents see on the screen. In addition to the 3D images just described, these include two-dimensional (2D) images, which represent cross-sections or "slices" of the body (like slices of a loaf of bread) that reveal details about internal organs such as the baby's heart. By contrast, the 3D images show the baby's outer contour, almost as if there were a miniature Hollywood film crew floating next to the baby in the mother's uterus, taking pictures and videos of the baby.

Your Travel Guide

We have written this book as a kind of visual travel guide to the world within a mother's body and to the journey of pregnancy. You will see what the baby looks like inside the womb at every stage of development. Explanations and diagrams will help you to understand how the baby grows and develops and to visualize the baby's current stage of development throughout your pregnancy. Furthermore, if you are pregnant and have had a sonogram, this book can help you understand your own ultrasound pictures.

The images in this book are unlike anything that previous generations of expectant parents have seen. Pregnancy is the only medical setting in which the doctor has two patients in one—the mother and her unborn baby. But until about forty years ago, the small, silent patient within the womb was invisible.

Then, tiny endoscopic cameras were used to take pictures of the external surfaces of the growing baby. But still, no pregnant woman could see a picture of her *own* unborn baby, and there was no way of looking at the baby's developing heart, kidneys, brain, or other structures while it was still in the womb.

About thirty years ago, ultrasound technology was introduced into many areas of medicine, including obstetrics. Suddenly, prospective parents could see pictures of their babies before birth. Over the intervening years, ultrasound has advanced dramatically. It is now able to show the unborn baby in far greater detail and in new ways, such as the striking 3D images now available. And the even more dramatic video ultrasounds now make it possible to watch and record the baby's movements inside the uterus. These videos show facial expressions, thumb-sucking, the mouth opening and closing, legs kicking, arms and hands exploring, and the heart beating. In fact, although the mother may not feel movement for the first four months or so of pregnancy, the baby is frequently in motion, with periods of rest lasting for only a few minutes. Even a full-term baby, ready to be born, generally rests for no more than thirty minutes at a time. (So that's why it is unrealistic to expect three-hour naps from a newborn!)

How Is Ultrasound Used?

A doctor may order or perform an ultrasound for a wide variety of reasons during pregnancy. It might be used to confirm an early pregnancy, to determine whether it is a multiple pregnancy (twins or triplets, for example), to assign the due date by assessing the *gestational age* (how far along the pregnancy is), to measure the size and rate of the baby's growth, to check the blood flow in the umbilical cord, or to make sure the baby's organs are developing normally.

While 3D ultrasound produces the pictures that are most irresistible to parents, it is 2D ultrasound that is most useful to the doctor because it shows the internal organs of both baby and mother. There are several other types of ultrasound images that can provide additional information to help the doctor evaluate the pregnancy. For this reason, a sonogram will often include 2D ultrasound images together with images of one or more of the other types of ultrasound. (The Appendix at the end of this book contains detailed explanations of the ultrasound procedure and the different kinds of ultrasound images.)

The ultrasound images and explanations in this book answer the questions of every pregnant couple: How is our baby growing? What does our baby look like now? What changes are happening this week? This month? How does ultrasound help my doctor make sure my baby is developing normally?

About Us

Who are we and why are we writing this book? We are two radiologists whose practices have been devoted to obstetrical ultrasound for more than twenty years. We wrote this book because we saw a need among our patients—a hunger for even the smallest detail about their unborn babies. In this book, we hope to share with expectant parents, as well as others interested in the miracle of pregnancy, a glimpse into the mysteries of the womb and an understanding of how the baby grows and develops before birth.

In addition to our practices, we are both professors of radiology at Harvard Medical School. We teach and see patients at the Brigham and Women's Hospital in Boston, a Harvard Medical School teaching hospital, where Peter is senior vice-chair of radiology and Carol is director of ultrasound and co-director of high-risk obstetrical ultrasound. Toward the end of this book, we have included stories that are typical of some of the patients we see, to show how ultrasound can be helpful in real life. These stories do not represent particular patients, but are composite portraits drawn from our years of experience.

Although this is our first book for general readers, we have coauthored textbooks, scientific articles, and book chapters on obstetrical ultrasound and lectured on the subject around the world. One of Peter's research interests is the analysis of fetal (unborn baby) growth and on mathematical approaches to medical decision making. (He also has a Ph.D. in mathematics from MIT.) Carol's research involves multiple pregnancies and the ultrasound diagnosis of pregnancy problems. She is currently involved in research on the use of surgery on the developing baby in the uterus to correct problems before birth.

Some patients ask us about the safety of ultrasound. Based on our personal experiences and the results of published research, we believe that ultrasound is a safe and valuable diagnostic medical procedure. Unlike x-rays or CT scans, it does not use ionizing radiation, which can cause damage to cells, especially the developing cells of a baby growing in the uterus. Ultrasound uses only sound waves—and only in tiny pulses, since most of the time is spent "listening" and interpreting the signals that are reflected back. The American Institute of Ultrasound in Medicine and a variety of other professional organizations have determined that there has been no documented detrimental effect of ultrasound in humans, despite the fact that it has been in general use for several decades. There is uniform agreement that the potential benefits of ultrasound justify its use for medical diagnostic purposes.

And now a bit about our personal lives: We are married—to each other—and between us we have five grown children. So, in addition to being doctors who perform thousands of obstetrical ultrasounds every year, we have also been the anxious parents on the other side of the ultrasound machine. Years ago, when we chose to specialize in ultrasound and to work with pregnant couples, it was because of the opportunity to share a significant and usually joyful life experience with our patients. While we are passionate about our research and teaching, it is the patient contact that we both treasure the most. With this book, we hope to reach out beyond our own patients to share with you the joy and the wonder of witnessing the creation of a new human being.

Acknowledgments

This book grew out of our experiences with our patients and their seemingly endless quests for details about their miraculous pregnancies. But books do not appear from ideas alone; they come from the vision and the hard work of many people. We are grateful to all those who helped us to translate our dream for this book into a reality.

We appreciate the support and encouragement of Anthony Komaroff, M.D., and Julie Silver, M.D., of Harvard Health Publications. In their dual roles as physicians and editors, they helped us navigate the world of trade publishing. We are also grateful to our editor at McGraw-Hill, Judith McCarthy. Her comments and suggestions were always right on the mark. No matter how well we thought we had written a chapter, her changes always made it better. We are indebted to Marisa L'Heureux, production director at McGraw-Hill, who was extremely helpful and knowledgeable in dealing with numerous production issues, including esthetic and technical matters related to image quality. We are very pleased with the appearance of the book, and for that we thank the cover designer, Tom Lau, as well as the interior book designers.

Obstetrician Lydia Lee, M.D., made a valuable contribution to the birth chapter by generously sharing her personal and professional experiences, as well as beautiful photos of her own newly delivered twins. We also want to thank the superb sonographers at Brigham and Women's Hospital for assisting in obtaining some of the ultrasound images used in this book.

Finally, we wish to thank our writer, Roanne Weisman. When we set out to write this book, we had the relevant medical and technical knowledge and extensive experience writing for a medical audience but had never written a book for a general audience. This limitation became apparent when we struggled to find the right words to explain concepts of ultrasound and pregnancy to readers without a medical background. This all changed when Harvard Health Publications connected us with Roanne. We have been amazed at how she can take a complex topic and make it not only understandable but also interesting and compelling to a lay audience. In addition, her upbeat attitude and good humor have made her a joy to work with. Without her collaboration in writing this book, it would still be an uncompleted dream instead of a finished product.

The Miraculous
Journey to a New Life

1

Marvelous Milestones: A Pregnancy Preview

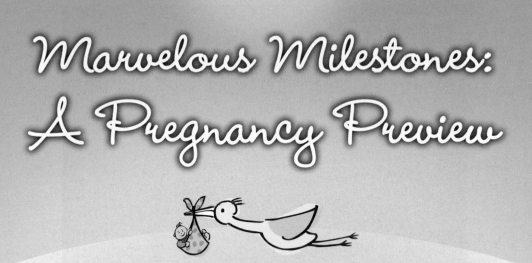

In a single nine-month sweep of time, a new and unique person emerges from a single cell. As if following the dramatic plot of a complicated script, cells divide, move up, move down, move sideways, and divide again to create the interlocking systems and structures of a human body. The creation of every new human being is a miracle, and most pregnant couples want to know as much as they can about their baby-to-be.

We're going to show you a detailed view of the development of a baby, from the time your body prepares for a possible pregnancy until a fully formed newborn loudly proclaims her entry into the world.

This first chapter is a pregnancy preview, an overview of some of the marvelous milestones of human development as revealed in ultrasound images. You will see many of these images reproduced later in the book, with more detailed explanations. But before you examine the minute details of the

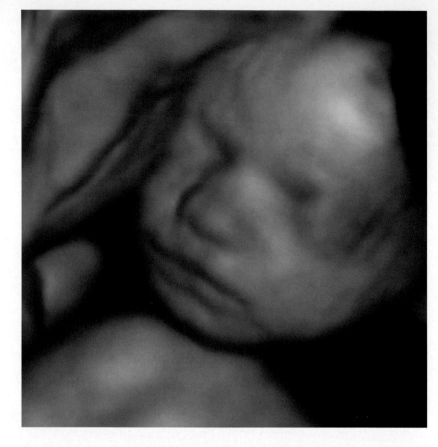

More than just a pretty face

Invisible in this 3D image are the complex internal structures of the brain, eyes, nose, and mouth.

developing heart, brain, abdomen, and limbs, take a moment here to appreciate the broad brushstrokes of nature as we give you some enticing glimpses of what is to come.

The image above, for example, shows the facial features of a baby girl fourteen weeks before her birth. Since this is a three-dimensional image, we do not see the busy activity going on under the surface of the skin. But in later chapters you will learn how the brain is becoming organized for thought, how the lungs are preparing for the first breath of air, and how the digestive organs are getting ready to receive the first swallow of milk.

Setting the Stage

The unborn baby girl shown on the previous page could not have appeared without careful preparation within the mother's body. Chapter 2 describes how the ovaries and uterus set the stage for the potential arrival of a fertilized egg each month. If fertilization occurs, within three to four days a small bundle of cells arising from the fertilized egg enters the uterus. In this nourishing environment, the group of identical cells develops into not only the baby itself, but also all of the supporting structures of the pregnancy, collectively called the *gestational sac*, shown in the drawing below. Please see "Pregnancy Terms" (page 6) for definitions of some important words used in this book, and then go on in this chapter to see a preview of the miraculous development of the baby throughout the pregnancy.

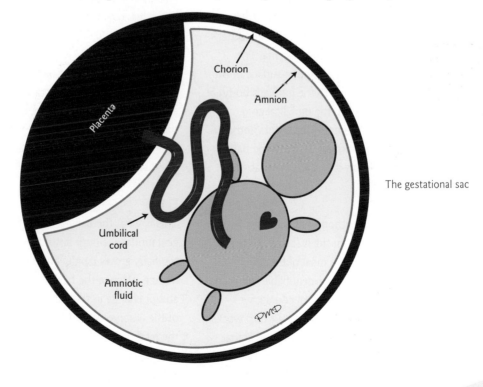

The gestational sac

Pregnancy Terms

Gestational Sac and Placenta

As seen in the illustration on page 5, the gestational sac is like a sturdy, water-filled balloon. Two membranes, the outer one called the *chorion* and the inner one called the *amnion*, enclose the gestational sac. Inside the sac is amniotic fluid, and floating within that are the baby and the umbilical cord. The umbilical cord (coming out of what will later be the baby's belly button) connects the baby to the placenta, a thickened part of the outer membrane. The placenta, which has blood flow from both the mother and the baby, is where mother and baby "communicate." Even though the blood systems of mother and baby are kept completely separate—never mixing together—oxygen and nourishment transfer from the mother's bloodstream to the baby's in the placenta. The mother's blood enters from the outer surface of the placenta (which is attached to the mother's body), and the baby's comes from the umbilical cord (which is attached to the baby). Nutrients and oxygen transfer from the mother's blood to the baby's blood to meet the needs of the growing baby.

Gestational Age

This is the traditional method of measuring the length of a pregnancy from the first day of the last menstrual period (LMP). For most of human history, the LMP was the only identifiable marker for the start of pregnancy. Now, of course, we know that conception takes place about two weeks *after* the first day of the last period. So the actual time since conception (*conceptual age*) is two weeks *less* than the gestational age. But doctors still use gestational age when measuring the length of a pregnancy. The "due date" is assigned as forty weeks (approximately nine months) after the LMP, because the average term delivery occurs at this point in the pregnancy.

Trimesters

We speak of pregnancy as being divided into three segments of about three months each. As commonly defined, the first trimester begins with the date of the last menstrual period and runs for thirteen weeks and six days thereafter; the second trimester covers fourteen weeks' gestation to twenty-five weeks and six days; and the third trimester covers the period from there until birth.

Embryo

This term describes the baby from conception until about ten weeks' gestational age (eight weeks after conception). During the embryonic period, the baby transforms from a small collection of cells to an organism with identifiable features and internal organs and structures.

Fetus

This is what the baby is called from ten weeks' gestational age until birth. During the fetal period, the baby grows rapidly and the internal organs mature. Despite the name change, there is no abrupt change in the baby to mark the end of the embryonic period and the beginning of the fetal period. For this reason, we prefer to use the friendlier term *baby* throughout the entire pregnancy.

The First Trimester

The first trimester is a period of rapid growth and development. It begins with a single microscopic fertilized egg cell that rapidly divides until it becomes a group of cells, still invisible on ultrasound. The baby, and the flicker of a heartbeat, first appear about four weeks after conception. At this point, it is less than a tenth of an inch long and has no identifiable parts, as shown below. (We have included labeled diagrams next to most of the ultrasound images in this book to give you a clearer idea of what you are looking at. On these diagrams, the baby is drawn using shades of blue, while all other parts—such as the uterus, placenta, and amniotic fluid—are drawn in black and white and shades of gray.)

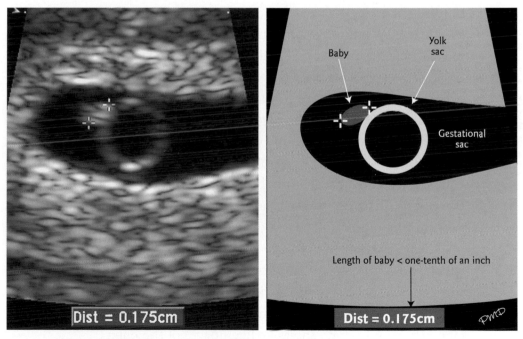

Early first trimester

An embryo at six weeks' gestational age

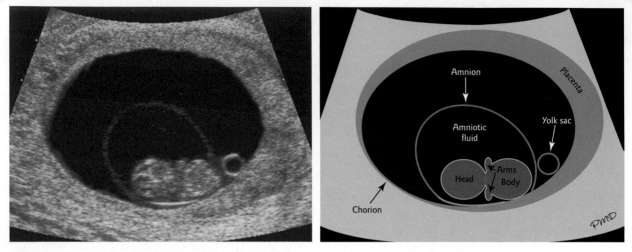

Middle first trimester: the appearance of form

At about nine weeks, the head is distinct from the body, and arms are beginning to develop. While not seen in this image, the baby's legs are at a similar stage of development.

Over the next several weeks, the baby grows and develops the beginnings of all of the organs and limbs. The transformation from a few cells to much more complex structures is spectacular. Within just thirteen weeks, the baby grows from a microscopic size to over two and a half inches in length and develops recognizable body parts and features, although the baby's organs must mature considerably before they can sustain life outside of the uterus. By the middle of the first trimester, the head, body, and beginnings of arms and legs can be seen, as is evident above. As the first trimester comes to a close, the baby's shape and facial features begin to resemble those of a newborn, as seen on the next page. (These two figures use the two kinds of ultrasound that you will be seeing throughout the book. The image above is a two-dimensional [2D] ultrasound, which shows cross-sectional views of the baby's body that look through the baby's skin surface into its internal tissues and organs. The ultrasound on the next page is a three-dimensional [3D] ultrasound, which shows lifelike images of the outer surface of the baby.)

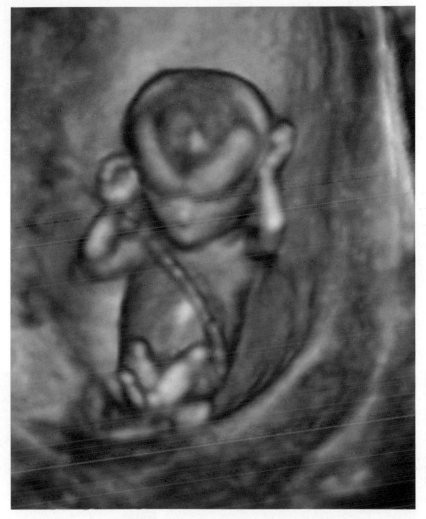

Late first trimester: the essential parts in place

In this 3D image of the late first trimester, the body's proportions are coming closer to what the baby will look like at birth. Note the umbilical cord floating across the chest.

Second and Third Trimesters: Function Follows Form

By the end of the first trimester, all of the baby's organs—or at least their essential parts—are in place. During the second and third trimesters, these organs grow larger and more complex and functional. Later we'll focus on how those individual body parts grow and develop. But first, here is a brief overview. The miracle of life unfolds!

Views of the face

The 3D image shows an aquiline nose and delicately open mouth (A). The 2D image shows not only the nicely rounded profile of the head, but also a glimpse of the brain and bones inside (B and C).

The Baby's Face: A Family Resemblance Already?

From early on, the baby's mouth, as you can see in these images, regularly opens and closes, as the baby swallows fluid and even sucks his thumb and fingers. The ultrasound below (A) is a 3D image of the face in profile, with the mouth open. The middle image below shows a profile of a baby lying on her back looking upward, using 2D ultrasound.

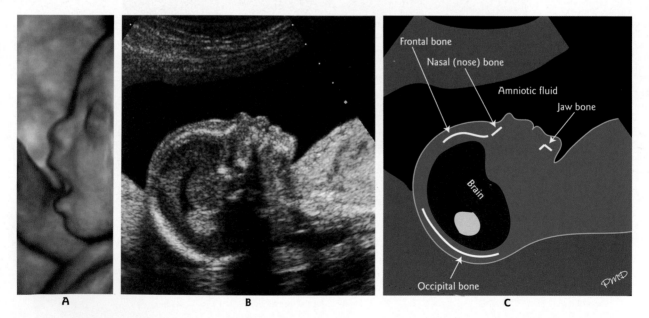

A   B   C

Frontal bone
Nasal (nose) bone
Amniotic fluid
Jaw bone
Brain
Occipital bone

Arms and Hands

The image of tiny human hands reaching out inside the uterus is perhaps one of the most powerful for prospective parents. The ultrasounds below show two views of arms and hands. The baby on the left looks almost as if he is waving hello! The 2D image on the right clearly shows the interior structure of the hand, including the three individual bones of each finger, shown as bright white areas.

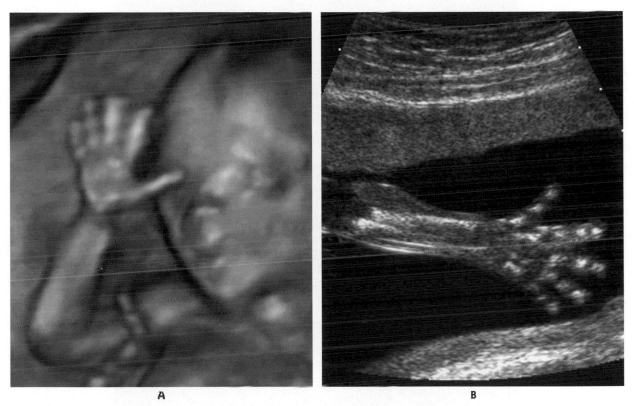

A   B

A wave from within

In A, note the umbilical cord draped casually over the shoulder.
And in B, the bright white areas in a 2D image show the finger bones,
as well as the growing bones of the forearm.

Legs and Feet

Here is a view of what is doing all that kicking inside! As you can see from the image, the baby and the umbilical cord can move into almost any imaginable position without causing problems.

Curl up and get comfortable

This 3D view is taken from behind, showing the lower spine, buttocks, and feet. Note the umbilical cord wrapped around the thigh.

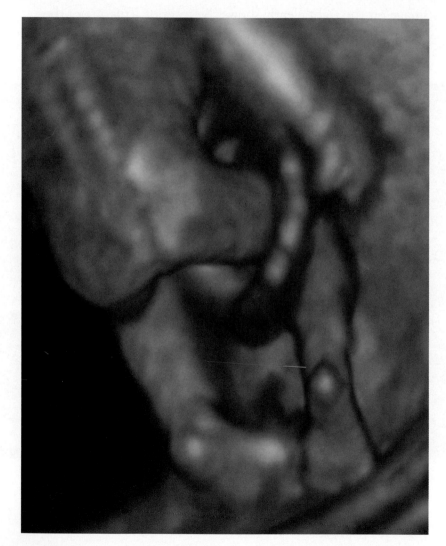

The spine and ribs

Spine: The Scaffolding of the Body Takes Shape

The 3D image above—using a special ultrasound technique that looks something like an x-ray—shows the interior structure of the skeleton, including the detailed structure of the vertebrae and ribs. Note the normal tapering of the spine toward the lower end.

Baby's Heart: The Beat of Life

The heart is first seen as a flicker at six weeks. By the second trimester, details of its structure are visible, including all four of its chambers. Because the heart is an internal organ, 2D ultrasound is the primary method for viewing it, another demonstration of the value of 2D ultrasound as a way of examining the inside of the baby's body. The ultrasound on the left is a cross-sectional view across the inside of the chest that shows the four chambers of the heart: the right and left atria, and the right and left ventricles. The labeled diagram on the right shows more clearly what you are seeing in the ultrasound image.

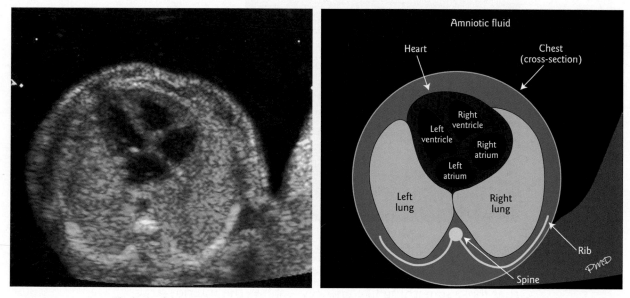

The heart of the matter

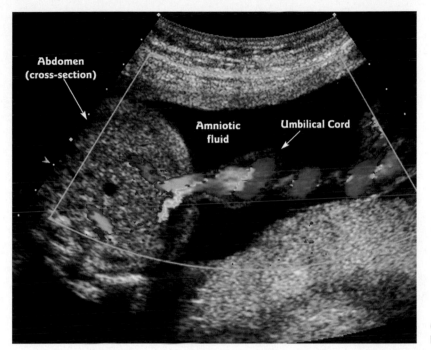

Umbilical cord: the baby's lifeline

Umbilical Cord: How Mother and Baby "Communicate"

It's through the umbilical cord, shown here, that the baby receives nourishment from the mother's body. (Review the sidebar on page 6 explaining pregnancy terms to see how this happens.) At birth, the cord is cut where it enters the abdomen, and that point becomes the belly button. In the Doppler image shown above, color shows blood flowing in the arteries and vein of the umbilical cord as it enters the baby's abdomen. (For details about Doppler ultrasound, please see the Appendix at the end of this book.)

Now that we have piqued your curiosity, it's time to continue our journey deeper into the world within.

2

Preparing for Pregnancy: The Body Gets Ready

While pregnancy is an incredible journey, what happens in your body *before* pregnancy is also an amazing process. From puberty until menopause, a woman's body prepares every month to become pregnant. This process begins in the brain, when the pituitary gland sends a hormonal signal to the ovaries, two small, oval-shaped organs buried deep inside the pelvis on either side of the uterus. And each month, in response to this signal, one of the ovaries releases a mature egg cell—ready to be fertilized by a sperm cell. In most cases, only one egg each month has the potential to become a new baby. The ovaries do not just produce the egg cell, they also release powerful hormones that cause physical changes in the uterus, preparing it to receive and nurture a newly fertilized egg. So whether or not a woman becomes pregnant, each month her body sets the stage for the arrival of a developing baby . . . just in case.

The Ovaries: Where It All Begins

While the main function of the ovaries is to produce egg cells, the ovaries also manage the monthly preparation for pregnancy by creating varying amounts of the female hormones estrogen and progesterone, which prepare the body to support the early growth and development of the baby. Estrogen and progesterone have other roles in the body—helping to keep bones and blood vessels healthy, for example—but it is the ovaries' role in pregnancy that is our main focus here.

The Monthly Egg Production Schedule

During the course of the menstrual cycle, the ovaries are dynamic, changing dramatically both in appearance and activity level, generating different amounts of hormones to prepare the body for a possible pregnancy. At the beginning of the menstrual cycle, when your period has just started, the ovaries are relatively quiet, and immature egg cells (*oocytes*) rest within the ovary, invisible to ultrasound. During the course of the cycle, as menstrual bleeding slows down, several of these immature egg cells begin to mature inside small, protective, nourishing, fluid-filled sacs called *follicles*. The image and accompanying diagram shown on the next page demonstrate a normal ovary with several small follicles during the early part of the menstrual cycle. (Although the fluid inside the follicles is clear, fluid appears black on ultrasound.)

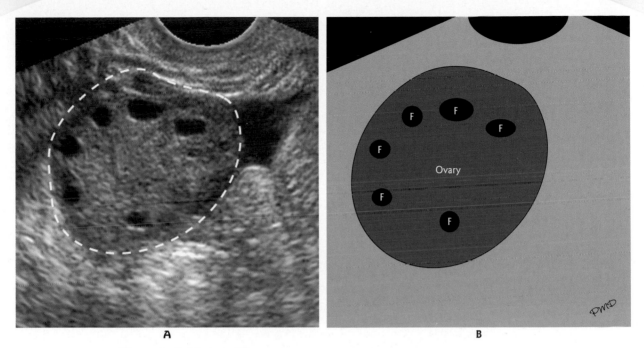

A   **B**

The potential for new life

The ovary, outlined by a dashed line on the ultrasound image (A), is oval in shape.
Each fluid-filled follicle, shown as a round or oval black shape with the letter *F* in B,
has the potential to release a mature egg cell, ready to be fertilized.

These follicles produce estrogen, which in turn causes the
bleeding of menstruation to stop. The increasing amount of
estrogen also prompts the lining of the uterus (the *endometrium*) to thicken in preparation for the possible appearance of
a fertilized egg.

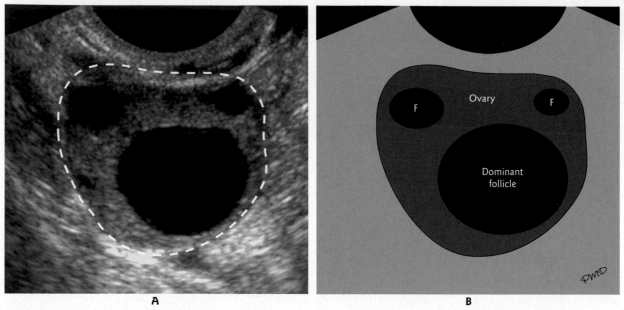

A   B

The chosen follicle

This ovary contains one large dominant follicle and two small follicles.

During the second week of the menstrual cycle, one of the growing follicles takes over, becoming larger than the rest, as you can see in the ultrasound shown above. This larger follicle is called the *dominant follicle* and is destined to produce the mature egg at the time of ovulation.

At the end of the second week, the egg inside the dominant follicle is mature enough to be released. Prompted by a surge of hormones from the brain, the follicle bursts open, releasing the egg in a process called *ovulation*. The egg, shortly after it is released, is snatched up by the moving, fingerlike projections at the end of one of the *fallopian tubes* and begins its journey toward the uterus. The fallopian tube (shown in the diagram on page 23) is a narrow passageway leading from the ovaries to the inside of the uterus, where pregnancies grow. While the egg is on its way along the fallopian tube it can become fertilized if it encounters sperm, and thus begins the nine-month journey of pregnancy. If the egg does not become fertilized, the follicle that produced it gradually shrinks in size and stops producing hormones, triggering the onset of menstruation.

A Pregnancy Begins: Hormone Overdrive

The follicle that released the mature egg is called the *corpus luteum* after ovulation. If fertilization occurs, the corpus luteum persists and may even get bigger during the first few weeks after conception in response to the hormone *human chorionic gonadotropin* (*h*CG) produced by the early pregnancy. During these important early weeks after conception, the corpus luteum provides essential hormones (especially progesterone) that prompt the uterus to provide increasing amounts of blood and nourishment to the growing baby.

Occasionally, an ovary creates more than one dominant follicle at a time, thereby producing two or more mature egg cells. This could result in multiple pregnancies—twins, triplets, or more—if more than one egg is fertilized in the fallopian tube. Multiple pregnancies are especially frequent in women undergoing fertility treatment because these women are commonly given drugs to stimulate the ovaries into producing several dominant follicles. (Part 4 contains more information about multiple pregnancies.)

The Uterus and Endometrium: Preparing a Home for the Baby

Most of the body's organs —such as the liver, heart, or pancreas—do not change significantly in form or function from day to day. The female reproductive organs, however, are different. Like the ovaries, the uterus changes dramatically during the menstrual cycle: every month it sheds its inner layer and then grows a new one, creating a fresh environment for a newly fertilized egg.

The uterus, located in the middle of the pelvis, is a hollow structure with a thick muscular wall. It has the potential to expand to hold a large baby (or babies) and then powerfully contract during labor and delivery. You can see in the drawing on the next page that the uterus looks like an upside-down pear. The lowermost portion of the uterus is the *cervix*, which is the opening to the vagina. The top of the uterus is the *fundus*. The main part of the uterus, lying between the cervix and fundus, is the *body*. The body is the region of the uterus that houses the baby during pregnancy.

Potential Space

The uterine body and cervix both have openings running down their centers called, respectively, the *uterine cavity* and the *cervical canal*. Both of these may be thought of as *potential* spaces: The uterine cavity remains closed or collapsed unless filled with menstrual blood or a baby, and the cervical canal is closed until the end of pregnancy, when it dilates during labor to allow the baby to emerge. The uterine cavity connects, through openings on both sides of the fundus, to the left and right fallopian tubes, which "catch" the newly released egg and funnel it into the uterus.

As the diagram shows, the body of the uterus consists of two layers: an outer, muscular layer called the *myometrium* (*myo* comes from the Greek word for "muscle") and an inner layer called the *endometrium* (from the Greek *endo* meaning "within"). The myometrium expands considerably during pregnancy and contracts during delivery to push out the baby.

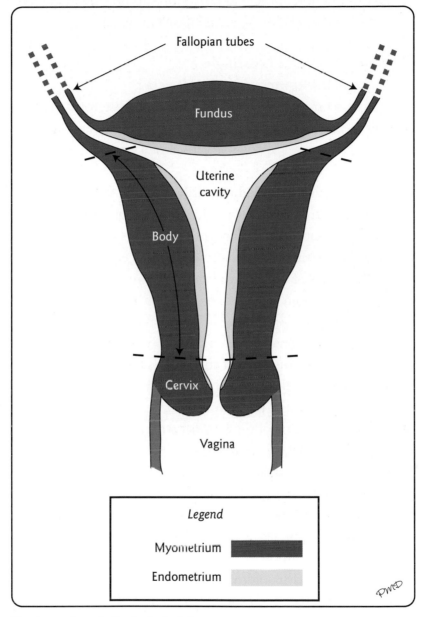

The uterus: a home for the developing baby

The main function of the endometrium is to prepare a nourishing home for the fertilized egg and developing baby.

Hormones at Work: Creating a Nourishing Environment in the Uterus

During the menstrual cycle, estrogen and progesterone cause changes in both the thickness and function of the endometrium, preparing for the possible arrival of a fertilized egg.

- **Days 1–4.** Vaginal bleeding during the first four days or so of the menstrual cycle represents the passage of endometrial tissue that had built up during the previous month.

- **Days 5–14.** After the menstrual bleeding ends, only a small amount of endometrial tissue remains. Over the next ten days, estrogen levels rise as the eggs begin to mature in the ovary, causing the cells of the endometrium to go into overdrive. The endometrial cells proliferate (grow) rapidly, so that this stage of the cycle is termed the *proliferative* phase.

- **Days 15–28.** By the middle of the cycle, about two weeks after the beginning of the last menstrual period, the endometrium is full of the extra blood vessels and special glands that would be needed during a pregnancy. Since these glands secrete fluid, the last half of the cycle is called the *secretory* phase. The uterus is now in a state of readiness, able to accept and nourish a fertilized egg if one arrives from the fallopian tubes. This timing of changes in the uterus is perfectly coordinated with what is going on in the ovary at midcycle: the mature egg is released from the ovary (ovulation) and is captured by the fallopian tube and transported into the uterine cavity.

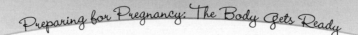

If fertilization has not occurred by the end of the fourth week, the uterus gives up its wait, as well as all of the extra blood vessels, glands, and other tissues it has accumulated, and the menstrual period begins. (While glands, which produce liquid substances that the body needs, usually remain permanently in the body, the special glands that are created in preparation for pregnancy die off in the absence of a fertilized egg and are flushed out of the body during the monthly period.)

Now that we have seen how the body gets ready to become pregnant, it is time to move on in our journey to the very beginning of a pregnancy: the first trimester.

The Journey Begins:
First Trimester

3

The Pulse of a New Heart: Early First Trimester

By the time a newly pregnant woman has missed her period, the rapidly dividing bundle of cells set into motion by fertilization has already become embedded within the lining of her uterus and begun the complex process of development. Within about two weeks after a missed period, an ultrasound image can capture the embryo and the beat of the developing heart. This chapter shows you the astonishingly rapid growth in the first eight weeks after conception (that is, up to a gestational age of ten weeks).

A reminder: we refer to a baby's *gestational age*, measuring from the time of the last menstrual period, rather than the time since fertilization—which actually occurs two weeks later. So the "six-week" embryo (baby in the early stage of pregnancy) has in fact been developing for only four weeks since fertilization occurred.

A Microscopic Biological Explosion

The union of egg and sperm at the moment of fertilization launches an explosion of biology within the future mother's body. But the pregnant woman typically remains unaware of the furious pace of activity inside her for several more weeks. By the time the woman has missed her period, two weeks after conception, the pregnancy can be detected by a blood or urine test but is still too small to be seen on ultrasound. Not until three weeks after conception (five weeks' gestational age) does it reach a size that is visible on ultrasound. So we can tell you what happens during the first three weeks after conception and only after that use ultrasound images to portray the pregnancy.

After ovulation, which occurs on about day fourteen of the menstrual cycle, the newly released egg is picked up by the fallopian tube and starts its journey toward the uterus, propelled by the tube's rhythmic contractions, called *peristalsis*. If sperm are present, fertilization may occur on the following day. The sperm and egg each have twenty-three chromosomes—half of what it takes to make a human being. When they unite, they each contribute their chromosomes to the newly formed cell, called a *zygote*, which now has the full human complement of twenty-three *pairs* of chromosomes—for a total of forty-six.

Even as it continues to travel toward its new home in the uterus, the zygote begins to grow, its cells rapidly dividing and multiplying. During this journey, the waiting uterus is already preparing to receive its new tenant. The uterine lining (endometrium) transforms, becoming an especially nourishing environment, helping to ensure that the early pregnancy "takes" and becomes well established. With the transformation of the endometrium into tissue especially rich in blood vessels, a new name is given to it during pregnancy: the *decidua*. The change in the lining is the direct result of a chemical signal from the corpus luteum—the remains of the ovarian follicle that originally released the egg.

By the time the pregnancy reaches the uterus, about three or four days after fertilization, the zygote has grown to a collection of about twelve to fifteen cells. By five or six days after fertilization, the collection of cells, now called a *blastocyst*, becomes embedded into the decidua in a process called *implantation*.

From Cells to Structure

An important aspect of this early stage of pregnancy is the process of *differentiation*: the transformation from a mass of indistinguishable cells to individualized cells that will have different parts, functions, and destinations within the baby's body. At the point of implantation, the cells of the blastocyst are fairly uniform, looking and acting very much alike. After implantation, however, groups of cells begin to vary in appearance and behavior. It is almost as if they have been assigned to different sections of an orchestra, with each group following its own part in a complex musical score, cued by the baton of an invisible conductor: some cells go on to form the membrane (lining) of the gestational sac, which will eventually surround the baby; others begin to form the placenta, which is attached at one end to the mother and at the other to the umbilical cord that will carry nourishment into the baby's body; and still others will become the baby's body—heart, brain, arms, legs, skin, and other organs.

Also noteworthy for this period is the rapid growth of the pregnancy. By day twenty-one—one week after conception and three weeks' gestational age—the pregnancy that has implanted in the uterus is the size of a pinhead. Two weeks later—at five weeks' gestational age—the pregnancy has grown to between one-tenth and two-tenths of an inch, and it finally makes its first appearance on ultrasound. We cannot yet see the developing baby, but we do see the "supporting cast": initially the gestational sac (containing the not-yet-visible baby) and, three to four days later, the yolk sac. (At this early stage of pregnancy, the clearest images are obtained through transvaginal ultrasounds, which are described in the Appendix.)

In the ultrasound image and diagram below of a five-week pregnancy, you can see the small fluid-filled gestational sac (about two-tenths of an inch in diameter), with nothing yet visible inside it—although you can be sure there is a great deal of activity going on!

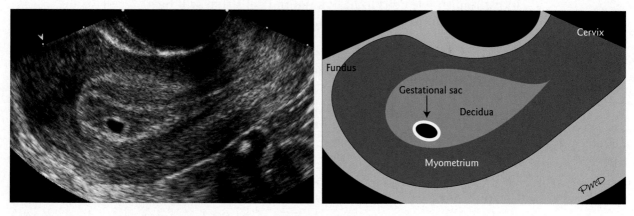

More than meets the eye: five-week pregnancy

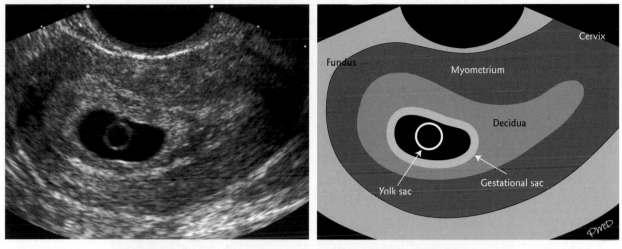

Fundus

Myometrium

Cervix

Decidua

Yolk sac

Gestational sac

Half a week later, a new structure can be seen: the yolk sac, as shown in the ultrasound image and drawing above. The ultrasound shows the yolk sac as a small circle inside the gestational sac. The yolk sac plays an important role in providing nutrients to the growing baby during the early weeks of pregnancy, before the placenta is sufficiently developed to take over this function.

By six weeks' gestation, the baby—the star of the show—is finally visible on ultrasound, first appearing as a tiny oval blip approximately a tenth of an inch in length, with a regular flicker of a heartbeat visible on the screen. Despite the baby's small size, the drama of the discovery is powerful for parents: for the first time, they are witness to the pulse of a new life inside the mother's body. The moment is special for doctors, too: even after more than two decades of medical practice, we still feel a fresh joy and excitement whenever we share the image of that first heartbeat with our patients.

Change in the picture: five-and-a-half-week pregnancy

There is a noticeable change in the appearance of the pregnancy between five and five and a half weeks of gestation. Now a yolk sac is clearly visible.

During the next three and a half weeks, the baby grows at an astonishing rate, as you can see in the ultrasound images and size chart diagram on these two pages. The baby grows from less than a tenth of an inch in length at six weeks, to a

The visible baby: six to nine and a half weeks

In each of these images, the baby lies between "+" calipers, which measure its length. The images show the size at six weeks (A and B), seven and a half weeks (C and D), and nine and a half weeks (E and F). In G you can see a comparison of sizes, showing the rapid rate of growth during this period.

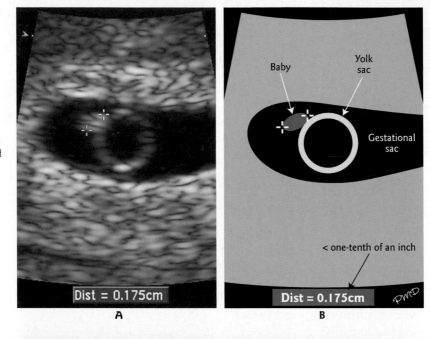

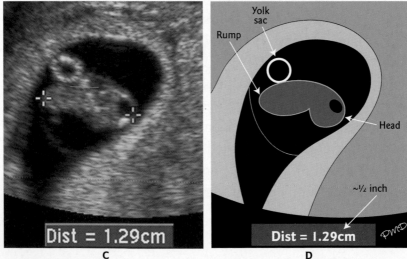

half-inch at seven and a half weeks, to one inch at nine and a half weeks: an increase of more than tenfold in just twenty-five days! The growth is even more striking when you realize that the measurement at nine and a half weeks excludes the legs,

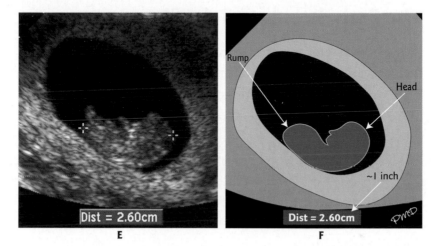

E

F

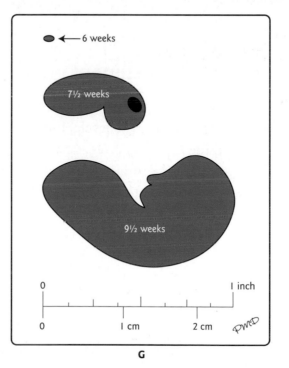

G

which have begun to form, since the standard way to measure a baby in the first trimester is from the top of the head to the bottom of the rump (the *crown-rump length*).

The Body Begins to Take Shape

If the big excitement during the first six weeks is the sight of the baby's heartbeat, the most striking event during the middle of the trimester is the appearance of identifiable human features. As you can see in the 3D images on the next page, the baby has recognizable parts such as head, trunk, arms, and legs by seven to eight weeks. These images also show that, even in the short time period between seven and eight weeks, considerable changes occur in the body shape and proportions, as the head develops a more rounded shape, the body elongates, and the neck straightens.

Taking Care of Baby: Protection and Nourishment

Growth is not the only activity going on during the first trimester. Complex systems are also developing to ensure that the baby receives all the necessary protection and nourishment to support this growth. The illustrations on pages 38 and 39 show how the mother's body protects and nourishes the developing baby in the middle of the first trimester. In the first of these illustrations, you can see the membranes, fluid, and other

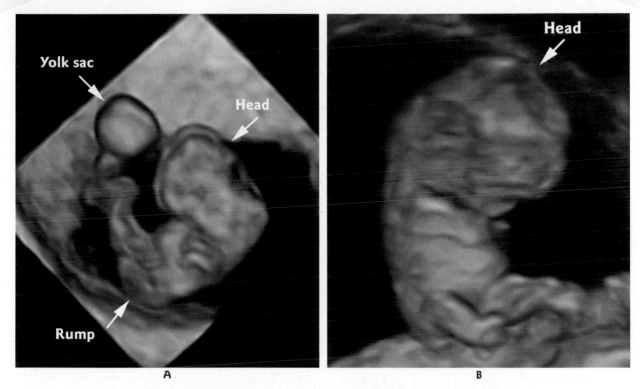

It's a head, an arm, a . . . !

Recognizable body parts are visible in the middle of the first trimester, as demonstrated in these 3D images at seven weeks (A) and eight weeks (B). Notice also the changes in body shape and proportions.

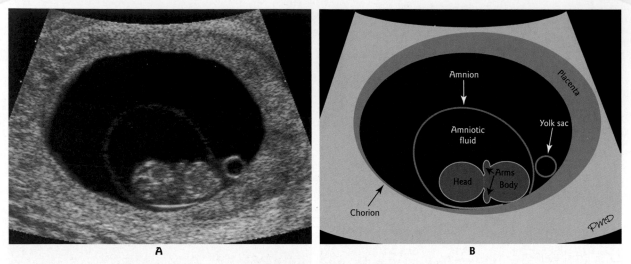

A   B

Floating in fluid

The 2D ultrasound image (A) and matching diagram (B) show the baby's environment in a nine-week pregnancy. Note the beginning formation of the baby's arms.

structures that protect and nourish the baby, and in the last you get a 3D view of the baby attached to the umbilical cord. As we mentioned in Chapter 1, there are two membranes surrounding the pregnancy and baby. The outer membrane, the chorion, has already begun to form the placenta, which provides nourishment from mother to baby via the umbilical cord. The inner membrane is called the amnion, shown as a thin white line. The amnion surrounds the baby and is filled with the amniotic fluid, within which the baby floats. As the baby grows, the space within the amnion gets larger and larger until the amnion meets and fuses with the chorion by the late first or early second trimester. But at this stage, the two membranes are still separated by fluid.

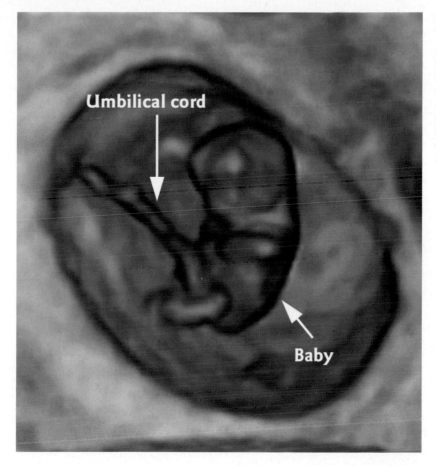

Umbilical cord

Baby

Another view, with depth

Here you see the baby's environment at just before ten weeks on a 3D ultrasound. The gestational sac is seen as a hollowed-out space within the mother's uterus.

So in less than eight weeks, what began as an indistinguishable mass of tissue has begun to take a humanlike shape. As if molded by a sculptor out of a lump of clay, the beginnings of arms and legs emerge and become recognizable. A head appears and begins to straighten—to rise up out of the body and sit on a neck. As we will see in the next chapter, the rapid pace of growth and development continues in the last four weeks of the first trimester.

4

From Structure to Function: Late First Trimester

Tripling in size, the baby grows from one inch at ten weeks' gestation to more than three inches by the end of the first trimester. By now, all organs and limbs are in place, the body is elongating, and the proportions are beginning to resemble those of a newborn. The rate of growth is astonishing and, as we explained earlier, the three-inch measurement does not even take into account the arms and legs. During weeks ten to fourteen, the baby's development takes a dramatic shift: from creation to growth; from structure to function. The baby's task over the next six months is to increase in size and maturity in order to be able to survive outside the mother's body.

The images tell the story: the ultrasound images below show you a common position of babies inside the gestational sac. They are almost always curled up with elbows and knees flexed, hands and feet close together (thus the origin of the term *fetal position*). The hands are often in front of the face, and the feet are sometimes crossed.

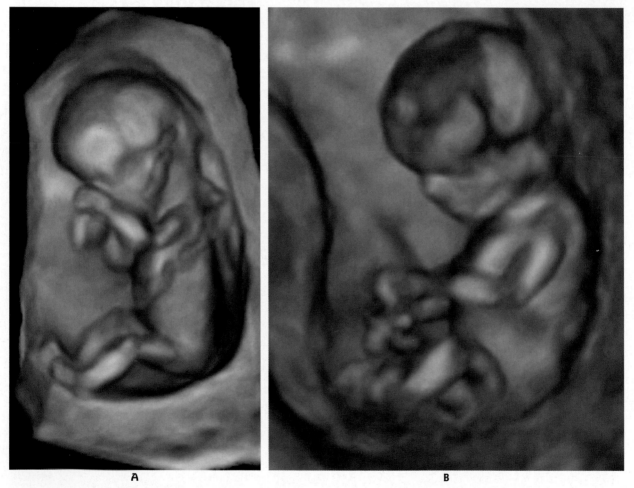

A   B

The fetal position

3D images of twelve- (A) and thirteen- (B) week babies

Dimensional Drama

To get an idea of the rapid growth as the end of the first trimester approaches, look at the 2D images below. These show the baby lying face up, and the size has been measured from the top of the head to the bottom of the rump. The surrounding black area is the amniotic fluid. The growth progression shows the body becoming longer, particularly in the trunk, and more proportional.

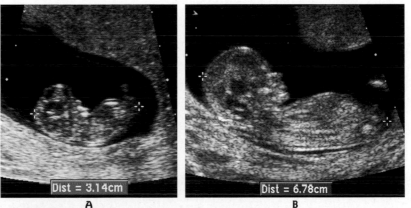

Dist = 3.14cm

A

Dist = 6.78cm

B

Floating progress

The first image (A) is a ten-week baby. Compare it to the thirteen-week baby in the second image (B). You can more fully appreciate the rate of growth by looking at the size chart (C).

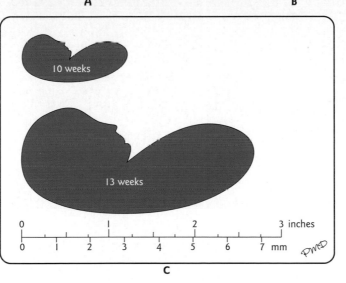

10 weeks

13 weeks

0   1   2   3 inches

0   1   2   3   4   5   6   7 mm

C

An Elaborate Network of Living Bone

By the late first trimester, distinct knees and elbows have formed, and the bones of the skeleton are beginning to ossify (harden). The process of *ossification* begins with the formation of cartilage, which appears in the shape of the bones to come. Then special cells "cement" the cartilage, calcifying it into an elaborate network of living bone, which gradually hardens and lengthens. On an ultrasound, hardened bone appears as bright white, as in the images shown below.

In the 3D image on the next page, you can clearly see the umbilical cord across the body, as well as arms, legs, and even the skull bones forming in the shape of "wings" at the top of the forehead. The *fontanel* (a soft, membrane-covered space between the bones at the top of the baby's skull) appears huge here. It will grow smaller as the bones enlarge to fill the space, but will still be present at birth.

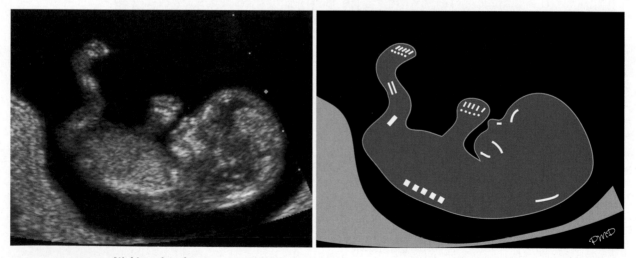

Kicking already

Even though the mother may not yet feel it, the baby's arms and legs are already in motion at twelve weeks.

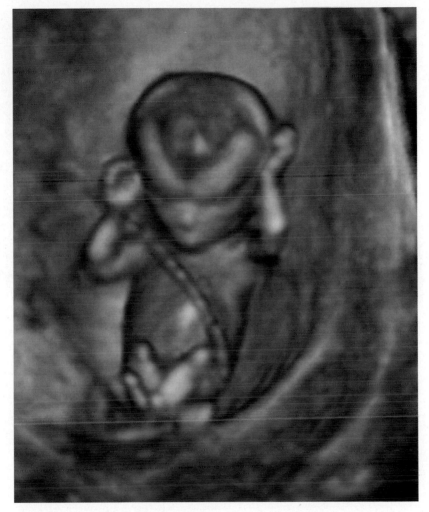

The over-the-shoulder look

The umbilical cord drapes casually over the shoulder and across the body of this thirteen-week baby. You can also see the tip of the nose and indentations where the eyes are developing.

Going with the Flow

There are two systems of circulation in the baby's body. One is the flow of blood through arteries and veins. The second is the *lymphatic* system, which carries fluid that seeps out of the arteries and veins back to the heart through tiny "tubules" and lymph nodes. This system helps to clear toxins out of the body

45

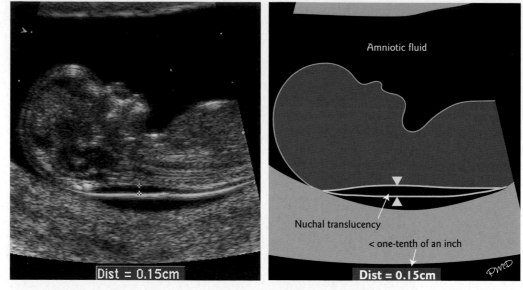

Making sure all is well

The nuchal translucency is seen on 2D ultrasound and highlighted in red on the corresponding diagram. This region is best evaluated with the baby lying face up (also giving us a striking image of the baby's profile). The thickness of the nuchal translucency, measured by "+" calipers on the ultrasound image and indicated by yellow arrowheads on the diagram, is one of the numerous ways that ultrasound is used to make sure the baby is healthy.

and reduce swelling. During the last few weeks of the first trimester, evidence of the lymphatic system is seen as a small amount of fluid inside the tissues at the back of the baby's neck. This fluid extends from the back of the head and neck into the upper back, and is seen as a dark region between two white lines on the 2D ultrasound above. The doctor uses ultrasound to measure the thickness of the black band, called the *nuchal translucency*, to make sure the baby is developing normally.

The Pathway of Nutrition

The umbilical cord, which carries nourishment from the placenta to the baby, enters the baby's body through the abdomen at the site that will become the belly button. The 3D ultrasound image on the opposite page shows the cord entering the baby. In this picture you can also see the yolk sac at the

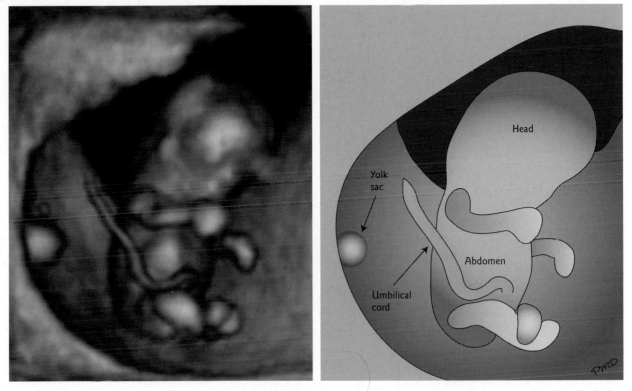

Yolk
sac

Head

Abdomen

Umbilical
cord

Feeding the baby

The umbilical cord
connects to the
twelve-week-old
baby's abdomen,
and the other end
of the cord (not seen
in this picture) is
attached to the
placenta, where it
receives nourishment
from the mother.

edge of the gestational sac. This is the last time we will see
the yolk sac before it disappears. It is no longer needed now
that the placenta has taken over the task of providing
nourishment to the baby.

With the end of the first trimester, the first part of our
journey through pregnancy is over. We now enter a new visual
landscape, in which we will discover individual parts of the
baby's body as they develop in preparation for birth.

The Growing Baby: Second and Third Trimesters

5

Don't I Know You? The Face and Head

Gazing at your baby's face before birth allows you to see far more than just recognizable facial features. You may also glimpse mercurial changes of mood. The power of 3D ultrasound invites us to experience as never before the baby's world inside the womb. Look at the 3D pictures on the next page, for example. The baby in image A appears peaceful and relaxed, while the one in image B seems amused. In image C, the baby is opening his mouth, probably to swallow amniotic fluid—one of the major activities of his day, helping to develop both muscles and the functions of swallowing and digestion. As they do after birth, unborn babies suck their thumbs, and even, as you can see in image D, engage in some less than polite nasal behavior!

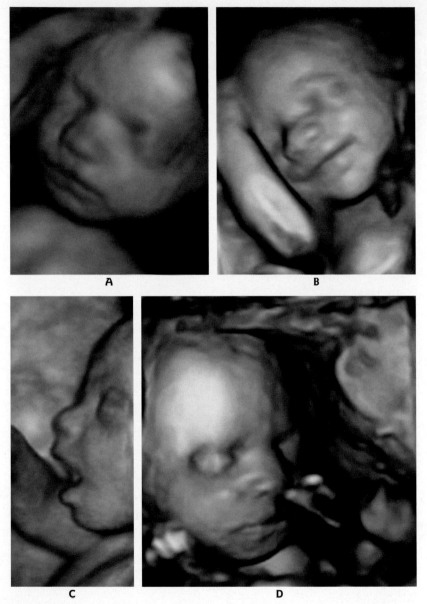

Baby's moods

Peaceful (A); amused (B); "Hey, you, out there" (C); a bit impolite (D)

What Is Going on Inside That Cute Head?

While the 3D pictures show the face in striking clarity, it takes 2D images to look through the face and into the brain, which is developing in both size and complexity. The 2D profile and its companion drawing below show the forehead, nose, upper and lower lips, chin, neck, and part of the chest. You can also see inside the head to the bones of the skull, which appear as the whitest areas. And looking deeper, you can see where the brain is forming. Even the lenses of the eyes can be seen on 2D ultrasound, though they are not visible on this image. The lenses move around frequently as the baby points her eyes in various directions, and the movement is especially vigorous when the baby is in rapid-eye-movement (REM) sleep, which we will talk about in greater detail in the chapter on the baby's movement.

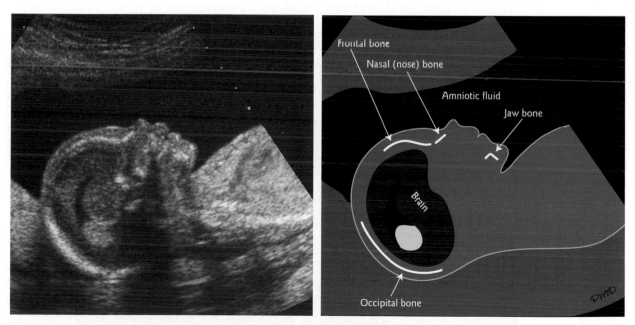

The baby in profile, with a view of the brain and bones inside the head

The Developing Brain:
The Essence of a New Human Being

The brain is the wondrously complex organ that houses the essential self of a human being. Using 2D ultrasound, which can peer inside the head and show cross-sections of the brain, we are able to see how this key organ grows and changes during pregnancy.

The image below, along with an explanatory companion drawing, shows some of the parts of the brain that we can see using 2D ultrasound. (Because of the way that ultrasound works, the bottom part of the brain always looks clearer and more detailed than the top part, but don't be alarmed! In reality the two halves of the brain are nicely symmetrical, as you can see in the diagram.) Shown are the major parts of the brain: the *cerebrum*, which is made up of two halves (the left and right cerebral hemispheres), and the *cerebellum*. The cerebrum is responsible for thinking, feeling, and controlling movement. The white line in the middle at the front, called the *falx*, is a membrane that divides the left and right hemispheres. The cerebellum, seen at the back of the head, is also responsible for

Thinking, feeling, and movement

The main parts of the brain—the cerebrum and cerebellum

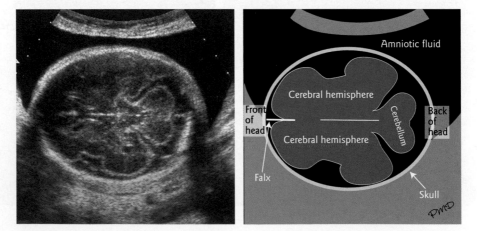

movement, but in a different way: this part of the brain coordinates the sequential movement of various muscle groups, allowing dancers and athletes, for example, to move their bodies in coordinated, graceful ways. This is the part of the brain that may help your child become a prima ballerina or a star pitcher!

The Brain's "Plumbing System"

The brain has an intricate "plumbing system" that circulates a continuous liquid bath of sorts for the inside and outside surfaces of the brain and the spinal cord, providing both shock absorption and protection. This liquid is called *cerebrospinal fluid*. Inside the brain, the plumbing system consists of four fluid-filled spaces called *ventricles*. The cerebrospinal fluid is produced within the ventricles by tissue called the *choroid plexus*, shown in the ultrasound below. After traveling through the ventricles, the fluid drains into the space surrounding the brain and spinal cord—the *subarachnoid space*—to bathe and protect the outside of the brain and spinal cord. The brain also has a network of arteries (not seen on this image) that carry blood to the brain cells to provide them with the oxygen and nutrients essential to life and growth.

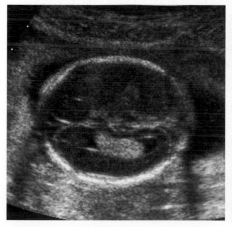

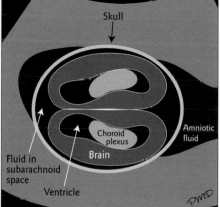

Protecting the precious brain

The choroid plexus produces cerebrospinal fluid, which fills the ventricles and subarachnoid space.

The Growing Brain

The baby's brain growth and maturation can be seen in a number of different ways: by its size, by its relationship to the support structures that protect it, such as the ventricles, and by changes in its surface.

Size. During the second and third trimesters, the length of the baby's head grows from one and two-tenths inches at fourteen weeks to nearly five inches at term. This represents a quadrupling in length and corresponds to a more than sixtyfold increase in volume. We will look at this growth in more detail in the chapter on the baby's measurements.

Relationship to Support Structures. A second way we can see evidence of brain development is by noting changes in the relative size of the "thinking" part of the brain—the cerebral hemispheres—compared to the support structures of the brain—the choroid plexus and the ventricles. At thirteen weeks, the support structures take up more than half the space in the skull, as you can see in A and B on the next page. By nineteen weeks, the thinking part of the brain is bigger than its support structures (C and D). And by thirty weeks, the thinking part of the brain is many times the size of the support structures (E and F).

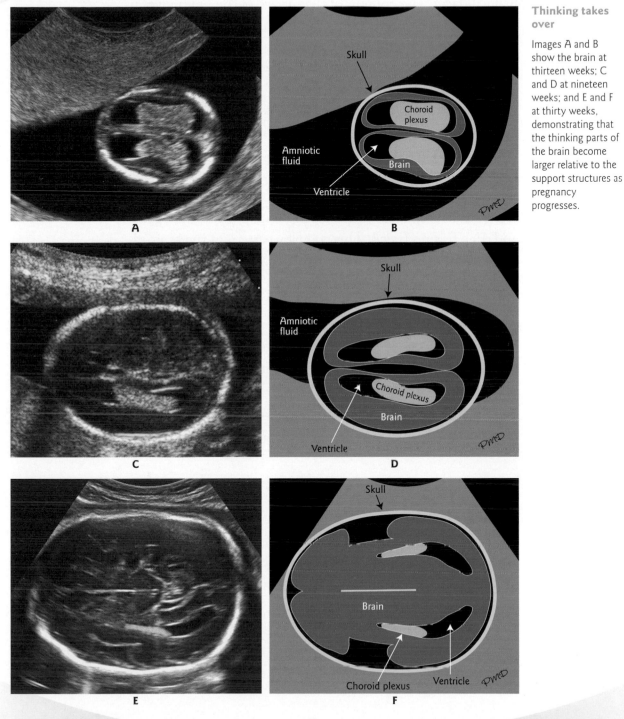

Thinking takes over

Images A and B show the brain at thirteen weeks; C and D at nineteen weeks; and E and F at thirty weeks, demonstrating that the thinking parts of the brain become larger relative to the support structures as pregnancy progresses.

Brain Surface. The contour of the surface of the brain gives us yet another way to see evidence of brain development. The surface is smooth during the second trimester, but it begins to fold into a "landscape" of hills and valleys as the baby progresses through the third trimester. The changes are shown in the illustration on the opposite page. At twenty-two weeks, the outer surface of the brain is very smooth, as you can see in A and B. By twenty-eight weeks, there is some folding of the surface, with the formation of bumps and furrows (C and D). Shortly before the baby is ready to be born, the terrain of the brain grows even more intricate, with bumps (known as *gyri*) and deep fissures (*sulci*). This complex pattern of the brain's topography, seen at thirty-four weeks in E and F, ensures that there is enough surface area within that small skull to hold the full complement of human brain cells.

Now that we have explored the face and head, let's move on in the baby's body. In the next chapter, we will look at the baby's chest, abdomen, and spine during the second and third trimesters.

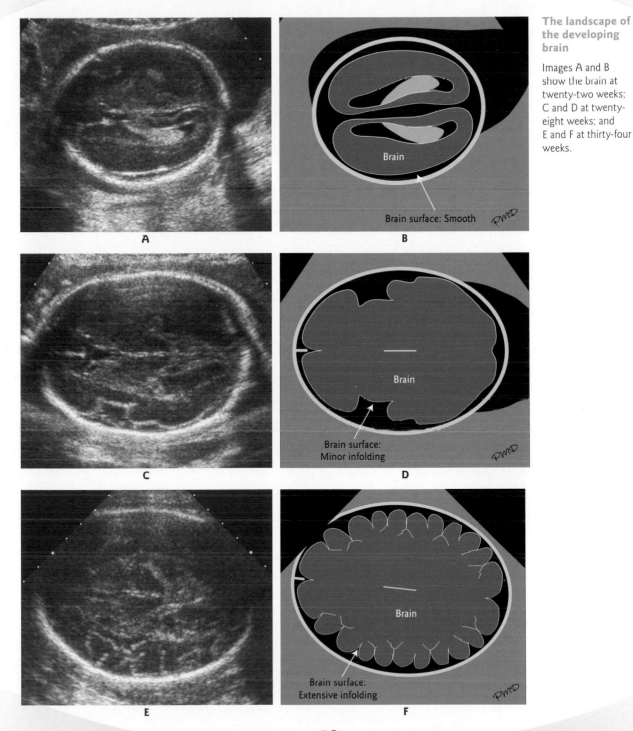

The landscape of the developing brain

Images A and B show the brain at twenty-two weeks; C and D at twenty-eight weeks; and E and F at thirty-four weeks.

A

B

Brain

Brain surface: Smooth

C

D

Brain

Brain surface: Minor infolding

E

F

Brain

Brain surface: Extensive infolding

6

A Hub of Activity: Baby's Body

That cute, round baby body houses a multitude of important organs and structures, all of which get bigger and more functional during the second and third trimesters. In this chapter, we peer inside the developing body to look at the chest, the abdomen, and the spine. All of these are parts of the baby's *trunk*, to which the head, arms, and legs are attached. The chest is in the upper part of the trunk; the abdomen and pelvis are in the lower part of the trunk; and the spine—with the attached ribs—runs the entire length of the trunk, providing both support and protection.

In the 3D image on the next page, we see the entire trunk, showing the ribs—here seen as partly bone (whiter areas) and partly cartilage—which are anchored to the spine in the back, and to the breastbone (sternum) in the front. The ribs and spine provide a rigid, protective cage around the lungs and heart.

Support and protection

This slightly rotated view inside the baby's trunk at nineteen weeks shows the ribs, spine, and pelvic bones.

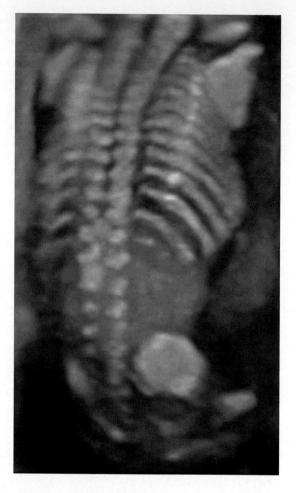

The Essence of Life: The Chest

If we think of the brain as the essence of the baby's personality, we might think of the chest as holding the essence of life: within it lie the lungs and the heart, together supplying the body with the breath and the circulating blood necessary for survival. Of course, the baby in the uterus does not breathe air, because all of the oxygen she needs comes from the mother's blood through the placenta. But that doesn't mean the lungs are inactive! At the beginning of the third trimester—about twenty-six weeks—the baby begins to practice the motions that will later become breathing.

The Lungs and Diaphragm: Controlled Movement

The chest and abdomen are separated by a thin muscle called the *diaphragm*, which completely seals off the chest from the lower part of the body, creating a sort of bellows effect. When the newborn baby is exposed to air and must breathe on her own, the diaphragm moves down, creating a vacuum, which draws air into the lungs through the mouth and trachea (the tube connecting the mouth to the lungs). This is how we breathe in. When the diaphragm moves back up, the air is expelled through the mouth or nose, and this is how we breathe out. During this process, the ribs and spine remain fairly rigid. Breathing is part of the *autonomic nervous system*, meaning that we do it automatically, even when we are asleep.

It is important for the baby, even while floating in his watery uterine environment, to practice moving the diaphragm up and down, as if breathing. These motions develop the muscles of the diaphragm and chest, as well as the signals from the brain that are needed to make breathing automatic. In fact, babies in the third trimester engage in these "breathing" motions for two to three minutes at a time, spending about a third of their time in this activity by the end of the pregnancy.

This breathing practice has a side benefit: As the lungs and diaphragm become stronger, they are able to pull some of the amniotic fluid through the baby's mouth and into the baby's lungs. The fluid then mixes with chemicals in the lungs, which are needed when the baby will breathe air. When the baby expels the fluid, it carries traces of these chemicals back into the amniotic fluid. Doctors can test the amniotic fluid for

Getting ready
to breathe

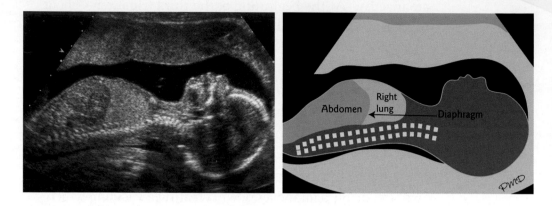

these chemicals to help determine when the baby's lungs are mature enough for birth.

The illustration above is a front-to-back lengthwise view of the lung and abdomen. The diaphragm is too thin to be seen here, but you can see that the right lung has a uniform pattern, compared to the abdomen, which looks less uniform because of the different organs within it.

The Heart: A Tiny Pump with a Big Job

The heart has four chambers: two ventricles, which pump blood out to the lungs and the body, and two atria, which pump blood into the ventricles to refill them. In the image on the opposite page, you can see all four chambers of a baby's heart at eighteen weeks—always a reassuring sight! The walls of the ventricles are thicker because they have to work harder than the atria. This image also shows a rib that is still partly bone and partly cartilage because it has not yet completely ossified. The sternum (breastbone) is not visible here because it is still made of cartilage and has not yet ossified. In the chest, the heart is always slightly to the left of the midline, which makes the right lung a bit larger than the left, because it does not have to share space with the heart.

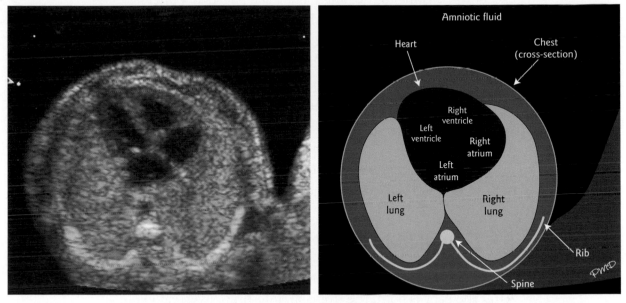

Labels on the diagram: Amniotic fluid · Heart · Chest (cross-section) · Right ventricle · Left ventricle · Right atrium · Left atrium · Left lung · Right lung · Rib · Spine

Everything is in place: heart, lungs, and ribs

The perfectly orchestrated circulatory system involves the precisely timed opening and closing of heart valves so that blood is directed to its correct destination. There is a *tricuspid valve* between the atrium and ventricle on the right side of the heart, and a *mitral valve* between the two chambers on the left side of the heart. These valves are closed when the ventricles pump blood out to the body to prevent blood leaking back into the atria. A fraction of a second later, when it is time for the ventricles to fill up again with blood from the atria, the valves open. Each complete cycle takes less than half a second.

Before the baby is born, the lungs contain no air. So the baby's blood receives its oxygen and nutrients from the mother via the placenta and umbilical cord (as will be discussed in a later chapter). However, the baby's heart still pumps and circulates blood within the baby, distributing the oxygen and nutrients throughout the body. The aorta, coming out of the left ventricle, carries blood to all of the baby's smaller arteries, except those going to the lungs. The *main pulmonary artery*, coming out of the right side of the heart, carries blood to the lungs.

After birth, when the lungs are full of oxygen-rich air, the right ventricle sends blood to the lungs to pick up oxygen. The blood then returns to the left atrium and travels to the left ventricle, which then pumps the oxygenated blood into the aorta to be distributed throughout the body. After giving oxygen to various parts of the body, the blood returns to the right atrium and the whole sequence begins anew.

It's Crowded in Here! The Abdomen

The lower part of the trunk houses the abdominal organs. After the baby is born, the stomach, intestines, liver, gallbladder, kidneys, and bladder will make it possible for the baby to digest the food she needs to nourish her body and eliminate toxins that could harm her. So after a look at a 3D outer view of the abdomen and attached umbilical cord on the opposite page, we will take a more detailed tour *inside* the baby's abdomen using 2D ultrasound.

The umbilical cord is the route through which the baby's blood—filled with oxygen and nutrients from the placenta—enters the baby's body, and through which the blood returns to the placenta for a nourishing "refill."

To continue our journey by looking inside the abdomen, we turn once again to 2D ultrasound. As in the chest, we can "see" into the abdomen using cross-sections, front-to-back lengthwise sections, or side-to-side lengthwise sections. These are similar to the views shown of the chest except that the cross-sections of the abdomen are located lower down the baby's body.

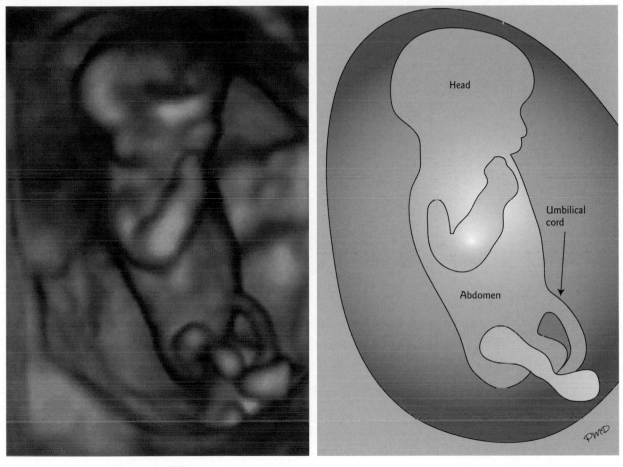

The cord of life

This image and diagram of a baby in the early second trimester shows the abdomen with the umbilical cord attached to what will later become the baby's belly button. Also visible are the head, right arm, and legs.

A full stomach

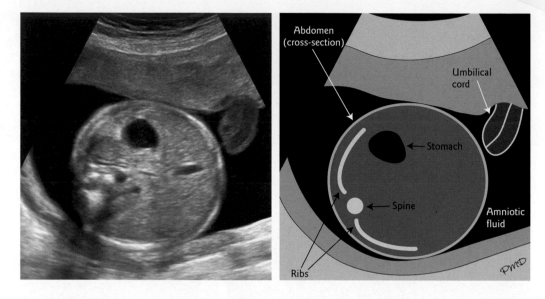

The Stomach

Our trip through the baby's abdomen starts at the top, where the first thing we encounter is the stomach. In the illustration above, we see the stomach in a twenty-three-week pregnancy. The stomach is full of fluid (which appears black on ultrasound), because the baby swallows amniotic fluid, which travels down the esophagus (the tube connecting the mouth to the stomach) into the stomach. This is a reassuring sight, because it tells us that the brain is sending the correct signals to the muscles involved in swallowing and that there is no blockage in the esophagus. If you watch these images in real time on the screen, you might see the stomach getting larger and smaller as fluid is swallowed and then drained out into the intestines.

The digestive system, which begins with the mouth, esophagus, and stomach, continues into the small and large intestines. Before birth, the intestines contain amniotic fluid that was swallowed by the baby. After the baby is born, the intestines absorb food and water for the body to use and send waste products out through the colon.

Near the stomach are two organs that will become more important after the baby is born: the liver and the gallbladder. The largest internal organ, the liver, is the body's main purifier, filtering toxic substances from the blood and producing the bile needed for healthy digestion. After birth, the teardrop-shaped gallbladder will store the bile.

The Kidneys and Bladder

The kidneys and bladder work together as the body's plumbing system, removing waste products and keeping the proper balance of fluids. In the ultrasound below and its accompanying diagram, you can see the two kidneys as oblong-shaped organs nestling on either side of the spine, which appears white because it is made of bone. As they filter the blood, the kidneys produce urine (a fluid seen as black in the ultrasound image). The urine then passes through tubes called *ureters* down to the

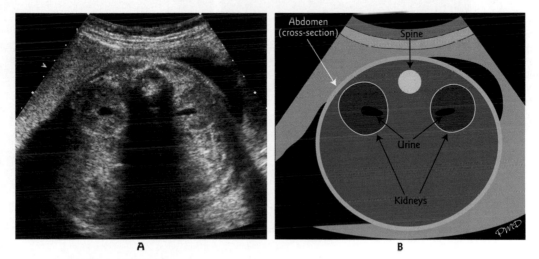

A   B

The plumbing system

These images show the kidneys of this thirty-three-week baby.
The dark vertical band in image A is a "shadow" cast by the spine.

bladder in the lower abdomen. From the bladder, the urine passes out of the baby's body through the *urethra* into the amniotic fluid.

Blood travels to the abdominal organs through a series of arteries. The baby's heart pumps blood through the *renal arteries* to the kidneys and through the *iliac arteries* to the pelvis. The iliac arteries give rise to several branches, including the *umbilical arteries*, which carry blood into the umbilical cord to be transported back to the placenta, where it deposits waste products and picks up oxygen and nutrients (described in greater detail in Chapter 12). The umbilical arteries disappear after birth. For a view of the umbilical arteries after they branch off from the iliac arteries, look at the color Doppler image and its diagram below. This image shows blood flowing through the umbilical arteries, which travel beside the bladder in the baby's pelvis to the umbilical cord.

Ever wonder how blood gets from the baby into the umbilical cord?

In this color Doppler image, the umbilical arteries are red because they contain blood flowing through the baby's pelvis and out into the umbilical cord.

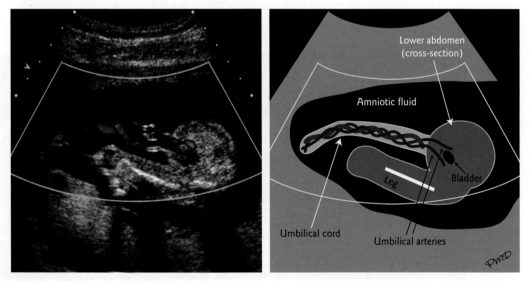

The Spine: Support, Protection, Communication Center

The spine is a collection of bones, called *vertebrae*, whose major function is to provide support for the body and protection for the spinal cord. The spine is a beautifully formed system that is both strong and flexible, extending from the head to the pelvis. It consists of twenty-nine vertebrae, which are stacked on one another with intervening firm, pliable "cushions" called *discs*. The stack of bones and discs is held together by ligaments. Each vertebra has a round block of bone in the front called the *vertebral body* and a sturdy bony ring in the back. The bony rings at the back of the vertebral bodies form an open column called the *spinal canal*, through which the spinal cord runs.

It is the discs and ligaments that allow you to arch or bend your back, while the rigid, bony vertebrae give you support and structure. In the developing baby, the vertebrae start out as cartilage and are gradually transformed into bone.

The spinal cord, housing long filaments of nerves coming from the brain, is surrounded by cerebrospinal fluid as it travels through the protective "tunnel" of the spinal canal. The cerebrospinal fluid is the same fluid that provides cushioning for the brain inside the skull. Because the spinal cord and its nerves are so fragile, they must be well protected, and that is the job of the spine, even as the baby grows inside the uterus.

You can think of the brain as the main computer server of the body, sending messages to and receiving information from local terminals in the organs and limbs. The spinal cord is like the router, directing information along nerve fibers (the body's ethernet cables), which branch out on both sides of each vertebra to the rest of the body. When the baby in the uterus kicks a leg, practices breathing, or swallows amniotic fluid, all of these activities are directed from the brain as it receives information and sends messages ("kick that foot as hard as you can") through the nerves of the spinal cord to the muscles controlling the baby's movements.

Not All Vertebrae Are Alike

The spine is not a stack of identical vertebrae. It is divided into four sections, each with a particular structure and function. The picture on the opposite page is a 2D image showing all of these sections in an eighteen-week baby: *cervical spine*, *thoracic spine*, *lumbar spine*, and *sacral spine*.

The Cervical Spine: Flexibility. The topmost part of the spine, extending from the base of the skull to above the shoulder blades, is the cervical spine, which consists of seven vertebrae. It is the most flexible part of the spine, allowing for rotation and movement of the head and neck, and it has the smallest vertebrae.

The Thoracic Spine: Protection. The thoracic spine is next, with twelve vertebrae extending from the shoulder blades to the back of the upper abdomen. The thoracic spine is noteworthy because each vertebra has a rib attached to it on either side. The ribs curve around from the back and converge in the front of the chest, where they join with the sternum to create a rigid cage that protects the heart and lungs.

The Lumbar Spine: Movement. Below the thoracic spine are the five vertebrae (the largest in the body) of the lumbar spine, located behind the abdomen. These vertebrae have no ribs

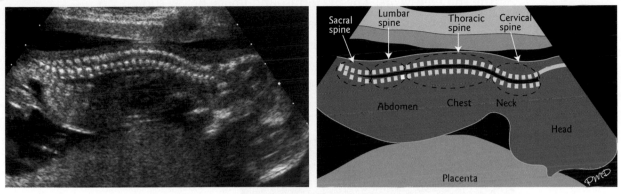

Sacral spine · Lumbar spine · Thoracic spine · Cervical spine

Abdomen · Chest · Neck · Head

Placenta

The spine: a beautiful piece of architecture

A 2D full-length image of a baby's spine at eighteen weeks. The baby is lying face down with all four sections of the spine visible.

attached to them and are more flexible than the thoracic vertebrae, providing motion in the lower back and waist for bending or turning side to side.

The Sacral Spine: Support. Finally, below the lumbar vertebrae are the five large vertebrae of the sacral spine, which are attached on either side to the bones of the pelvis, a cup-shaped structure of bone that protects the organs in the lower abdomen. (In the pregnant woman, the pelvis protects the intestines, bladder, and uterus with the baby inside, providing a solid support to hold up the growing abdomen.)

From Cartilage to Bone: The Spine Takes Shape

The process of bone formation is a gradual one. At first, each vertebra consists of a complete ring of cartilage around the spinal cord. As the pregnancy progresses, bone begins to replace the cartilage in three separate "ossification centers" in each vertebra. In the 2D image above, you can see two of these three centers in each vertebra, with the bone showing up as bright white. Gradually, these bony sections grow closer and closer together, but the cartilage is not fully replaced by bone in the vertebrae until the child stops growing, some time during the teen years. The 3D ultrasound image below shows the spine of an eighteen-week baby. You can see each of the ribs attached to the thoracic vertebrae. Also clearly visible are the cervical vertebrae in the neck, the lumbar vertebrae in the lower spine, and the sacral vertebrae, flanked by the supportive pelvic bones.

The strengthening spine

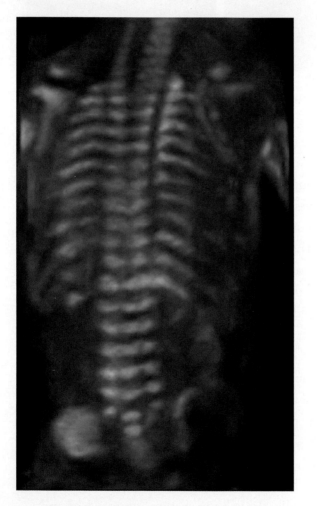

Protecting the Spinal Cord

An important function of the spine is to protect the delicate spinal cord and the nerves inside it. In the cervical spine, the spinal canal (the bony ring that surrounds and protects the spinal cord) is wider than in the thoracic spine, and it continues to narrow as it moves down the back. This is because in the neck area, very few nerves have branched out to the body, so the spinal cord is thickest here. As the spinal cord descends, more and more nerves branch out to arms, legs, and internal organs, so the cord gradually becomes thinner. The spinal cord within the spinal canal ends in the lumbar spine, just below the belly button. Below that point, the spinal canal is filled with nerves that float freely in cerebrospinal fluid until they exit toward their destinations in the pelvis and legs.

In accordance with the ever-diminishing number of nerves within it, the spinal canal gets progressively narrower until it tapers to an end in the lower sacrum. This tapering is demonstrated in the 2D image below of the spine in a nineteen-week baby with an accompanying diagram.

Now that we have looked closely at the baby's chest, abdomen, and spine, let's branch out to the arms and legs, seeing how they develop and how the baby moves around inside the uterus.

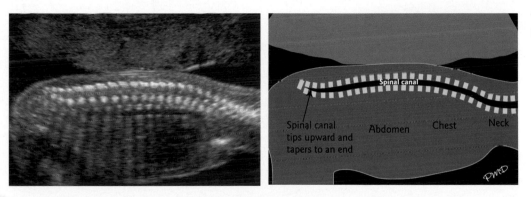

Tapering of the lower spine

Shake It Baby! Arms, Legs, and Movement

Feeling the baby move—what used to be called *quickening*—is one of the most reassuring and thrilling experiences a pregnant woman can have. Where there is movement, there is vigorous life! Being able to see the baby move on an ultrasound screen adds to the thrill. One of the advantages of ultrasound is that we can see movement before the mother even feels it.

When the mother does feel movement, some time during the second trimester, it is usually the result of an active baby's arm or leg. So let's begin by looking at the development of the *extremities*—arms and legs.

Arms and legs begin to form in the early first trimester. At first, they are small bumps protruding from the baby's trunk. By the middle of the first trimester, they look more like flippers than what we think of as arms and legs, yet all of the essential parts are in place. Each of these flipperlike shapes is divided into the three sections that will become a fully formed arm

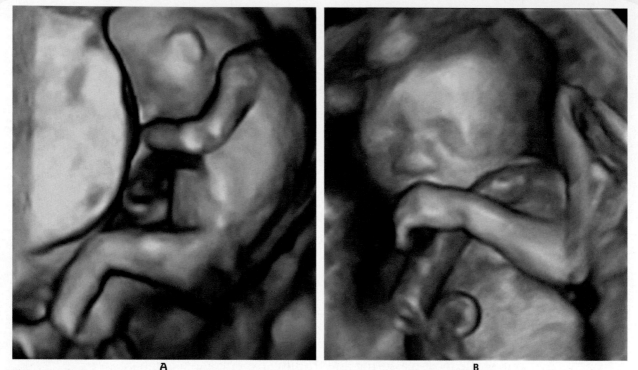

A   B

This series of 3D images shows a nice collection of arms and hands, some with detail of tiny baby fingers. Image A shows the shoulder and upper arm at eighteen weeks; B shows the forearm at twenty-two weeks; and C and D show the hands at twenty-seven weeks.

(upper arm, forearm, and hand) or leg (thigh, calf, and foot), with cartilage foretelling the positions of future bone. The bones consist of the single bones of the upper arm and thigh, the two parallel bones of the forearm and calf, and a collection of small bones in the hands and feet.

During the second and third trimesters, each section of the arms and legs continues to elongate simultaneously. The process of growth is beautifully simple. The main part of the bone is called the *shaft*, which is ossified (meaning that calcium has been deposited within it to make it hard and strong). At either end of each bone is a cartilage structure called the *epiphysis*. The shaft and epiphysis are connected by the *growth plate*, which produces new bone to lengthen the shaft. The

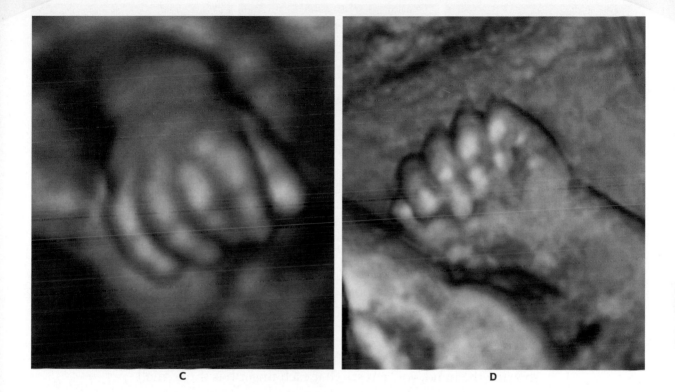

C   D

growth plates will remain in place until the late teenage years, when the child finally stops growing.

Let's take a visual tour of the arms and legs. The 3D images on these two pages show the arms and hands of a number of second and third trimester babies, from the shoulder down to the fingers.

The images on the next page are 2D views of the arm and hand that allow us to see the bones developing inside them. The single bone in the upper arm is called the *humerus*, and the two parallel bones in the lower arm are called the *radius* and the *ulna*. The parallel structure of bones in the forearm allows for greater rotation while still giving support and stability to the hands. The shafts of these three bones show up as

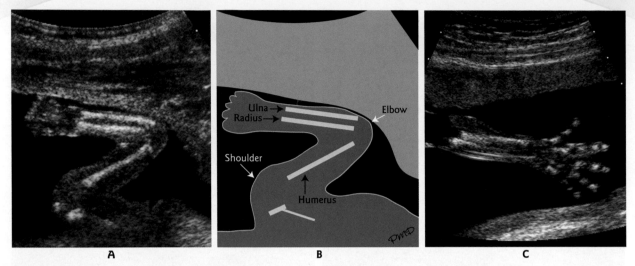

A   B   C

Inside the arm and hand

The baby in A has a gestational age of nineteen weeks; the baby in C is twenty weeks.

bright white structures because they have ossified. The dark areas in the shoulder, elbow, and end of the forearm represent the cartilage and growth plates at the ends of these bones, which allow the shafts to continue to grow longer. In the image showing the hand, you can see that each finger has three small bones and the thumb has two—the same as you will find if you examine the fingers and joints in your own hands! This image also shows that the bones in the fingers ossify earlier than those in the palm (the same as we will see for the bones in the toes in relation to those in the sole of the foot).

Getting Ready to Walk: Baby Legs and Feet

These images of graceful and beautiful legs and feet hardly need explanation. The 3D images on the opposite page show babies of different ages in colorful poses, and the 2D images and diagram on page 82 show the bones in the leg of a

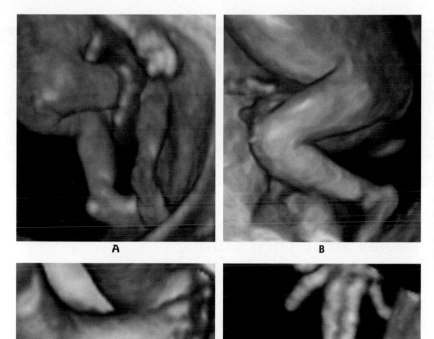

A

B

C

D

Posing for the camera?

These babies seem to be cooperating to show us their legs and feet in 3D. Note the umbilical cord wrapped around the thigh in A (sixteen weeks), the well-formed, muscular-looking leg in B (nineteen weeks), the demurely crossed ankles in C (thirty-three weeks), and the hand and foot together in D (thirty-two weeks).

nineteen-week-old baby and the foot of a twenty-seven-week-old baby. Although it is not visible on this image, there is actually a second bone in the calf to provide flexibility and support. Note also the red arrowheads at the ends of the shaft of the femur in the diagram; these show how that bone is measured. As we will discuss in the chapter on baby measurements, doctors often use the length of the femur to date the pregnancy and to make sure that the baby is growing normally.

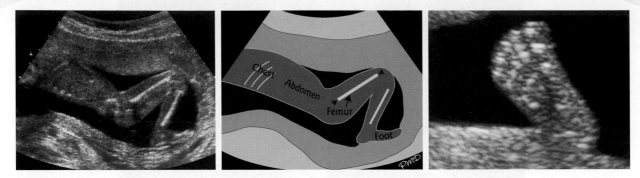

A look inside the legs

Notice the knee and foot pushing against the wall of the uterus.

Movement Is Life: Babies Strut Their Stuff

Even though most women do not feel movement until about eighteen to twenty-two weeks, and sometimes as late as twenty-five weeks, ultrasound tells us that babies move well before that. And they move much more than arms and legs: they open and close their mouths, turn their heads from side to side, roll over, and, as you will see, even wink!

Ultrasound shows movements as early as eight weeks. Although we cannot show you actual movement in this context, we can show you sequences of still images that were taken moments apart. Your imagination will have to do the rest! The images on the facing page, for example, show movement in a nine-week pregnancy through a series of three still images.

The Baby's Sleep "Personality"

Despite the eagerness of prospective parents to see or feel constant movement, the baby actually spends a great deal of time sleeping—about twenty to thirty minutes at a time. At thirty-two weeks of pregnancy, for example, the baby is asleep more than half of the time. Even in the uterus, babies have different sleep "personalities" or patterns. As mothers who have

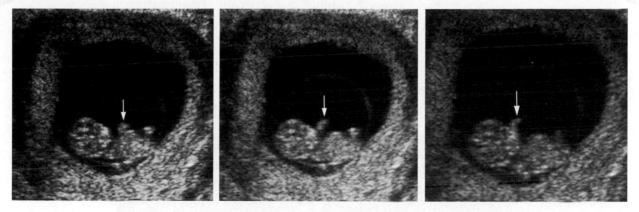

A fascinating recent discovery is that babies in the uterus sometimes engage in REM (rapid eye movement) sleep, which is associated with dreaming after birth. This has been verified by a number of scientific studies, including ultrasound studies based on observation of movement of the lens of the eyes. So an interesting question arises: is the baby dreaming? We have no way of knowing the answer—at least not yet.

had two or more pregnancies often notice, the sleeping pattern can vary considerably from one baby to another.

A wave from within

This nine-week baby can be seen moving his arm (shown by an arrow) in a waving motion from his chest up to his face. The pregnant mother cannot feel any movement yet.

Movement Means Good Health

Baby movement in the uterus is one way that the doctor assesses whether the baby is in good health. As we all know, when we feel sick, we don't feel like moving around much. The same thing is true for the baby during pregnancy. So, when we perform an ultrasound in the third trimester and don't see any movement for a while, we might make a buzzing sound next to the mother's belly. If the baby is asleep, he will wake up with a startle! A healthy baby will move his body in several ways: flexing and extending arms and legs, bending his back, stretching, rolling from side to side, opening and closing his mouth and eyes, even sucking his thumb. It is generally thought that these movements are important for stimulating muscle growth, keeping joints flexible, and strengthening bones. Sometimes mothers wonder whether a very active baby in the uterus means a hyperactive child later in life, but there is no evidence for this kind of a connection.

A future musician?

This twenty-eight-week baby bends and extends her tiny fingers.

Baby aerobics

In the first image, this fifteen-week baby has extended his arm; in the second, he raises it as if lifting weights.

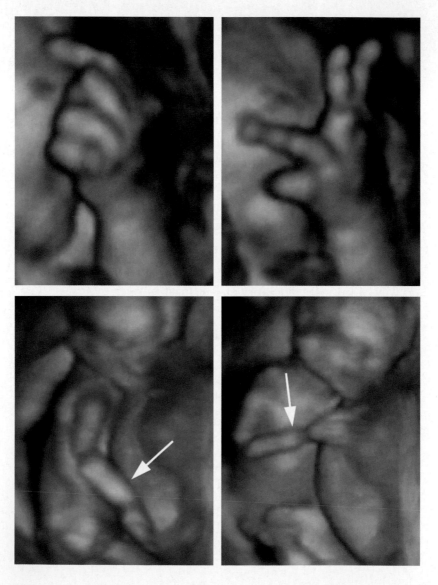

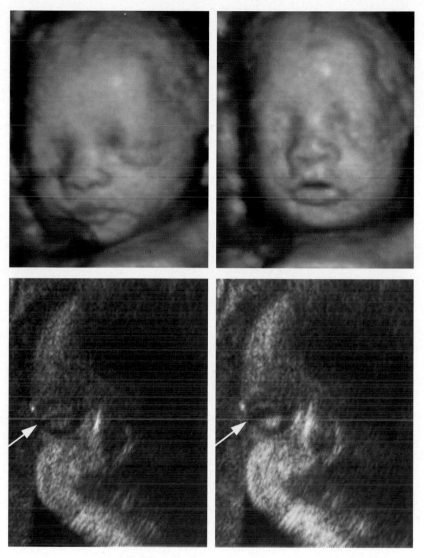

Say aaaahhh!

As this twenty-eight-week baby opens his mouth, you can see the umbilical cord lying next to the head.

A secret baby joke?

This thirty-six-week baby seems to be winking at us!

The images on the preceding page and above show you different movement sequences involving the arms, legs, and face. Enjoy your baby's movement. It is a sign of good health!

Now that we've seen how (and what!) babies move, let's go on to learn how to tell the boys from the girls. (It's easier on ultrasound than you might think!)

8
Telling the Girls from the Boys: Sexual Organs

Much has been written and said about the differences between males and females in everything from physical strength to social interaction. However, we are more alike than you might realize: in fact, during our first few weeks in the uterus, we are exactly the same. For the first half of the first trimester, all babies—whether destined to be boys or girls—have identical sexual equipment (called *genital ducts*), with the capacity to make either male or female organs. These organs start out as three small bumps between the baby's legs, one in the middle and two on either side of it.

The big change happens in the latter part of the first trimester. Babies with one X and one Y chromosome (boys) produce testosterone (male hormone), which prompts the bumps to develop into male sexual organs. The bump in the center elongates to become a penis, while the two bumps on either side grow downward to join under the penis to form the

What little boys
are made of

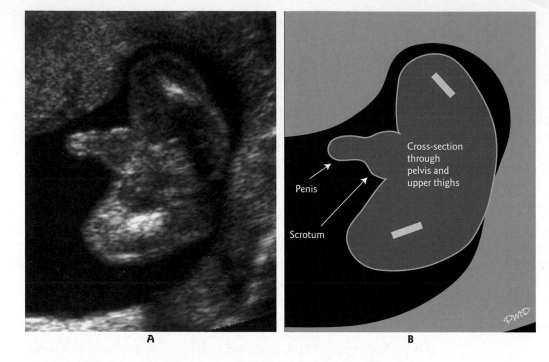

scrotum. The testicles develop inside the lower abdomen and, some time shortly before or after birth, descend to their permanent home in the scrotum.

The penis and scrotum are seen in the 2D image and diagram above of an eighteen-week boy. The testicles have not yet descended into the scrotum. A 3D image and diagram of a fifteen-week boy (C and D on the next page) provide another view of the penis and scrotum. The testicles, each surrounded by fluid in its own separate compartment, are visible within the scrotum in the 2D image and diagram of a thirty-six-week boy (E and F).

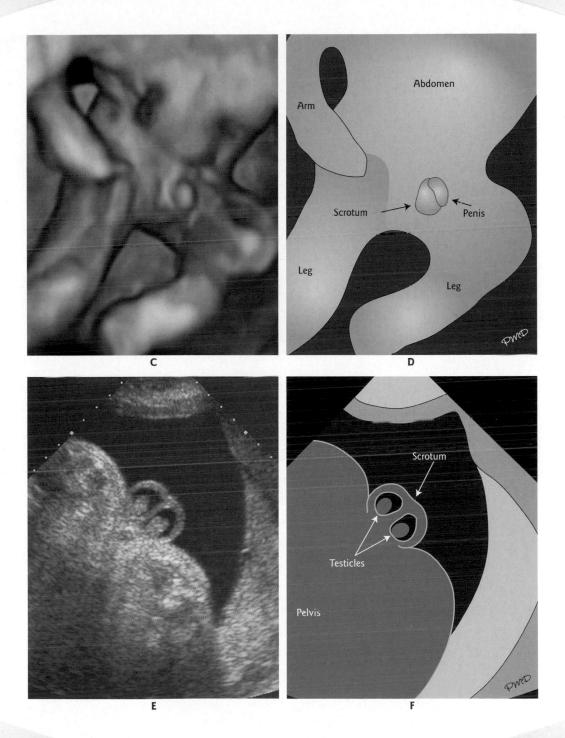

C

D

Abdomen

Arm

Scrotum → ← Penis

Leg

Leg

PMD

E

F

Scrotum

Testicles

Pelvis

PMD

Girl power

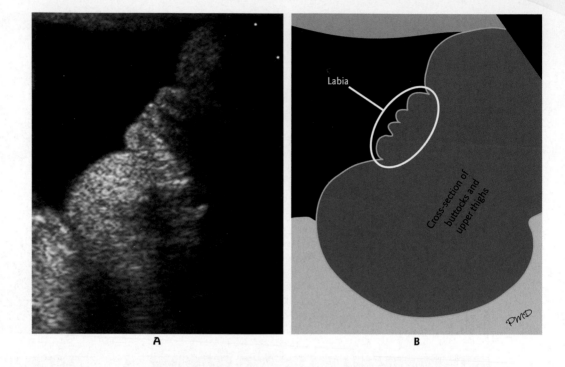

Labia

Cross-section of buttocks and upper thighs

A   B

Babies with two X chromosomes are girls. In the absence of testosterone, the bump in the middle remains small and the ones on either side become the folds known as the labia, which surround the entrance to the vagina. They do not fuse together like the scrotum. Instead of testicles forming in the lower abdomen, the baby girl develops ovaries. And these, of course, stay within her pelvis permanently.

The 2D and 3D images here show the development of female sexual organs. The labia are visible in a 2D image of a thirty-five-week girl above and a 3D image of a thirty-week girl on the next page. The tiny ovaries, hidden inside the pelvis, are not visible on ultrasound.

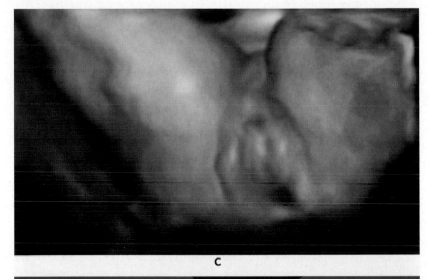

C

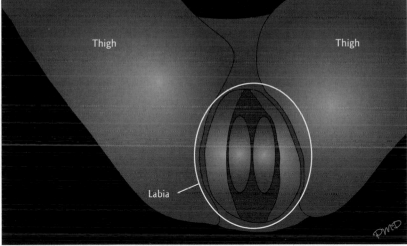

Thigh

Thigh

Labia

D

Our final group of images in this chapter shows you an important biological function: urinating. Not glamorous, perhaps, but necessary for the creation of new amniotic fluid, since (as we will see in Chapter 12) amniotic fluid consists mainly of the baby's urine. The images below show the flow of urine coming from both a girl (A) and a boy (C). The flow of urine from the girl is shown by color Doppler, which, as you will recall, is an ultrasound technique that shows the movement of fluid, including blood or urine.

Not potty trained yet

Baby urination is essential for maintaining the correct amount of amniotic fluid around the baby. Images A and B show a stream of urine (seen on a color Doppler image) coming from a twenty-two-week girl. (The other colored area shows the flow of blood in a nearby artery.) Images C and D show a thirty-four-week boy urinating into the amniotic fluid, with the penis and scrotum clearly visible.

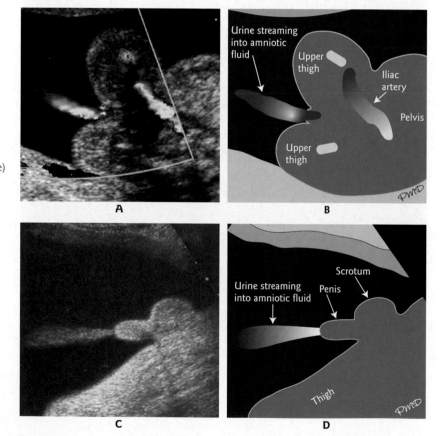

We move now from our contemplation of sex differences to differences of another kind: size.

9

Size Matters: The Baby's Vital Statistics

Imagine yourself at a cocktail party—the kind where people stand around in small groups and make clever comments to one another. If you were to see someone very tall, you certainly would not say, "Oh, you must be quite old!" You also would not say to a short person, "My, how young you look!" One reason you would not do this, aside from its rudeness, is that you would be wrong. In adulthood, size has no correlation to age, as you probably know if you have ever craned your neck to reprimand a teenaged boy who looms a foot above you!

As we move backward in the life span, however, size relates more and more closely to the age of the person. So, if you tried to predict the age of a toddler by his size, you would be fairly accurate. The farther back in time you go, toward birth, the more accurate your age-by-size guess would be. And continuing to reverse the progression of time, into the uterus and through the nine months of pregnancy, back to the first days after conception, using the baby's size to determine age approaches almost scientific precision. In the third trimester, determining age by size is accurate to within two to three weeks. In the second trimester, the size of the head and femur will predict the age to an accuracy of within one to one and a half weeks. And in the first trimester, the crown-rump length will accurately predict the baby's age within three to five days.

It is the use of these measurements before birth that is the subject of this chapter: why do we measure the unborn baby and how do we do this? Earlier in this book, we discussed the crown-rump measurement and nuchal translucency, which are measurements used in the first trimester. Here, we will focus on measuring the baby during the second and third trimesters.

Why Measure?

Because of the correlation between the size of the baby during pregnancy and its age, an important use of measurements is to date the pregnancy—to determine the baby's gestational age accurately. Ultrasound measurements, in most cases, are more accurate than the last menstrual period (LMP) for determining the gestational age. This is because women do not always remember the exact date of their LMP, and because the length of the menstrual cycle varies from woman to woman. Accurate information about gestational age is important to the doctor, since a number of pregnancy management decisions are based on it, including the choice of whether to stop premature labor or when to perform a cesarean section.

Measurements can also help the doctor check on the baby's health in a number of ways. By combining measurements of the baby's head, abdomen, and femur, the doctor can estimate the weight of the baby. Estimates of the baby's weight, combined with age, confirm that the baby is growing normally and help the doctor identify problems before they become serious. If the baby is too small for his age, for example, there might be a problem with insufficient nourishment coming from the placenta. This might lead the doctor to deliver the baby early so that nourishment can be provided by mouth or intravenously.

Measurements have other medical uses as well. For example, in some situations measurements of parts of the baby's body, including the thickness of the skin behind the baby's neck and the length of the bone in the nose, can give the doctor valuable information about the baby's genetic makeup.

Ultrasounds are done for medical indications, but measurements can also help answer a question that parents often have: how big is my baby right now? While many books and websites about pregnancy provide graphs and tables that list the average size of a baby at various stages of pregnancy, ultrasound goes one big step farther by giving parents specific information about the size of their own baby. For example, a woman who is thirty weeks pregnant can go to one of these books and find out that the average weight for a baby at this stage is two pounds and fourteen ounces. But if she has an ultrasound at that time (not simply to satisfy her curiosity, but for a medical indication), she might find out that her baby is estimated to weigh three pounds and five ounces. While this is an estimate, and not a precise determination of the baby's weight, it is more accurate than a table of averages.

Measuring Up: How It Is Done

On ultrasounds performed in the second and third trimesters, measurements are routinely done on specific body parts. These routine measurements include the length and width (or circumference) of the head and abdomen, and the length of the femur. The head and the femur measurements are used to estimate the baby's age, and in the third trimester the three measurements are combined to estimate weight. The diagram below shows what is routinely measured in the unborn baby.

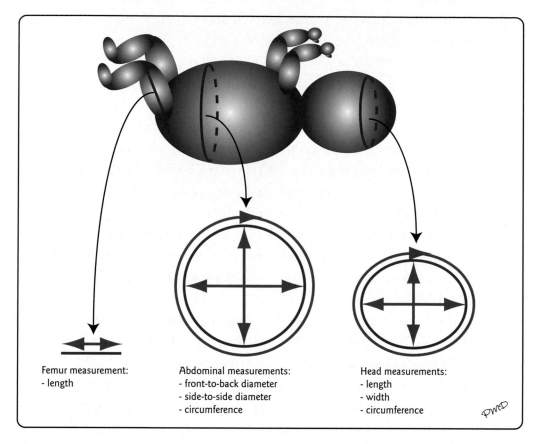

Femur measurement:
- length

Abdominal measurements:
- front-to-back diameter
- side-to-side diameter
- circumference

Head measurements:
- length
- width
- circumference

Sizing you up

The red lines show the structures being measured, and the green lines show the measurements that are taken in each area.

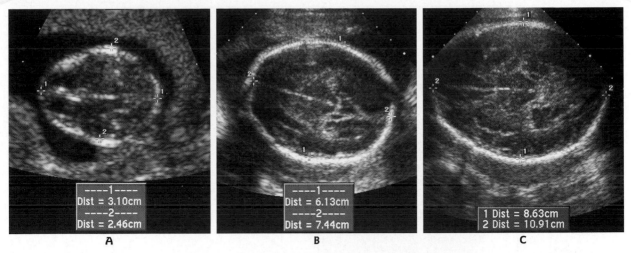

A

----1----
Dist = 3.10cm
----2----
Dist = 2.46cm

B

----1----
Dist = 6.13cm
----2----
Dist = 7.44cm

C

1 Dist = 8.63cm
2 Dist = 10.91cm

A Closer Look at Measurements

The ultrasound images in this chapter show you measurements of the baby during the second and third trimesters, but they are not to scale: we have magnified the images in order to make the areas being measured more visible, and the degree of magnification is greater for images done earlier as compared to later in pregnancy. To give you a better idea of how the baby grows, we have included diagrams that directly compare the measurements at various stages of pregnancy. In the 2D images on this page and diagram on the next, for example, you can see that the head nearly quadruples in length, width, and circumference from the beginning of the second trimester to the end of the third trimester.

More room to think!

The length of the head increases from one and a quarter inches at fourteen weeks (A) to three inches at twenty-five weeks (B) to four and a quarter inches at thirty-five weeks (C). These dramatic changes are illustrated in the comparative size chart (D).

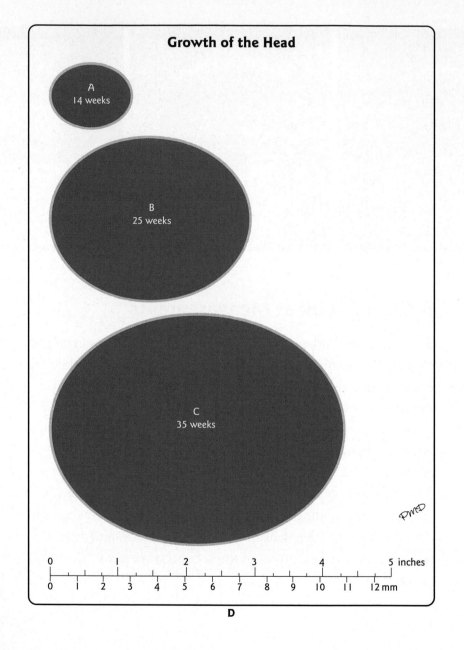

Growth of the Head

A
14 weeks

B
25 weeks

C
35 weeks

PMD

0   1   2   3   4   5 inches
0   1   2   3   4   5   6   7   8   9   10   11   12 mm

D

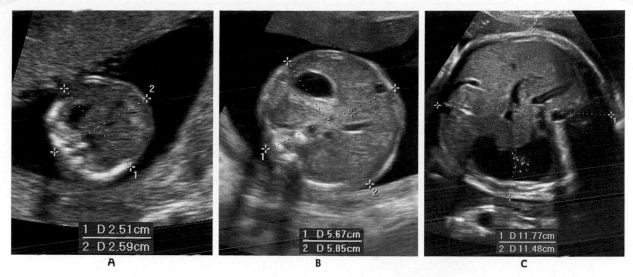

| 1 D 2.51cm |
| 2 D 2.59cm |

A

| 1 D 5.67cm |
| 2 D 5.85cm |

B

| 1 D 11.77cm |
| 2 D 11.48cm |

C

The series of 2D ultrasounds above and the accompanying diagram on the next page show that the abdomen grows even faster than the head, more than quadrupling in diameter during the second and third trimesters. It is measured from front to back and side to side. (Chapter 6 shows some views of the internal organs of the abdomen.)

A growing tummy

The diameter of the abdomen increases from approximately one inch at fifteen weeks (A) to two inches at twenty-three weeks (B) to four and a half inches at forty weeks (C). The diagram (D) shows the comparative sizes.

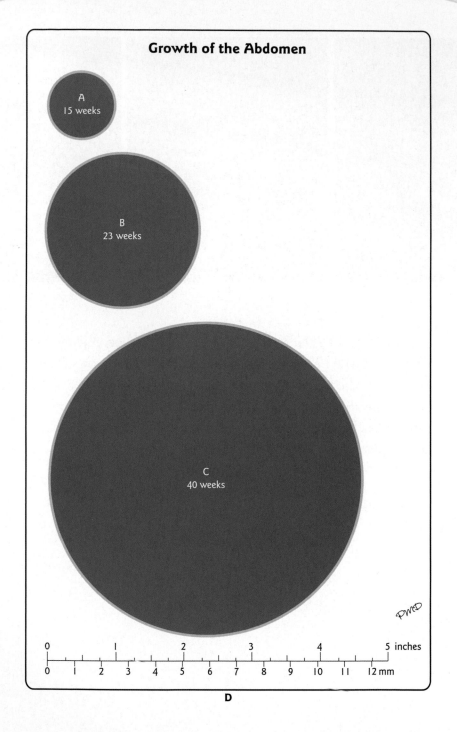

Growth of the Abdomen

A
15 weeks

B
23 weeks

C
40 weeks

PMcD

0   1   2   3   4   5 inches
0 1 2 3 4 5 6 7 8 9 10 11 12 mm

D

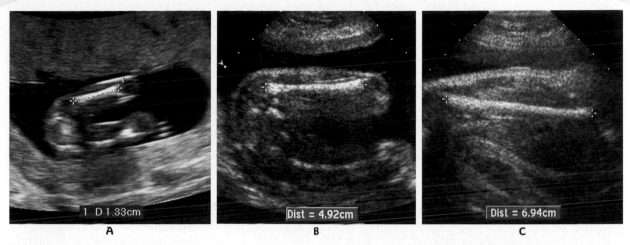

1 D 1.33cm	Dist = 4.92cm
A	**B**

Dist = 6.94cm

C

Lengthening legs

The length of the femur increases from approximately one-half inch at fifteen weeks (A) to nearly two inches at twenty-five weeks (B) to a little more than two and a half inches at thirty-five weeks (C). The diagram (D) shows the comparative sizes.

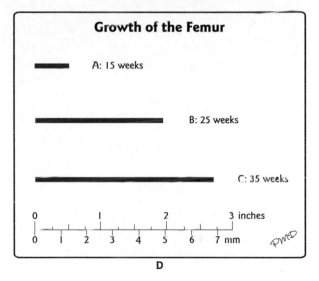

Growth of the Femur

A: 15 weeks

B: 25 weeks

C: 35 weeks

0   1   2   3 inches

0   1   2   3   4   5   6   7 mm

D

The femur grows very quickly, as well, increasing fivefold in length during the second and third trimesters, as you can see in the ultrasounds and diagram shown above. The thick white stripe in the ultrasound image is the bone, surrounded by the muscles and skin of the thigh. (More details about the legs and arms are discussed in Chapter 7.)

In addition to the head, abdomen, and femur, doctors sometimes measure other parts of the body to answer specific questions about whether the baby is developing normally. Among the parts sometimes measured are the nuchal fold shown below, nasal bone on the next page, humerus (upper arm bone), and cerebellum (part of the brain). The nuchal fold is a measurement of the skin and soft tissues at the back of the neck; measuring it is analogous to measuring the nuchal translucency in the first trimester.

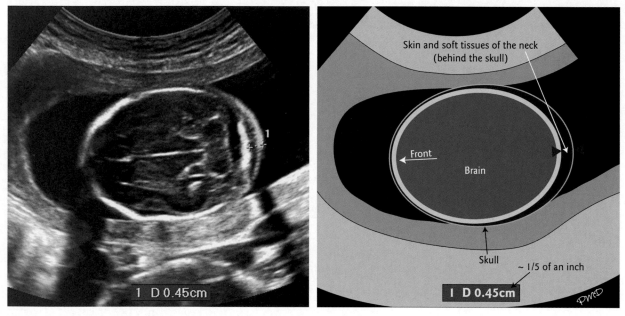

Nuchal fold

The skin and tissue at the back of the neck measure approximately one-fifth of an inch, a normal thickness in this nineteen-week baby.

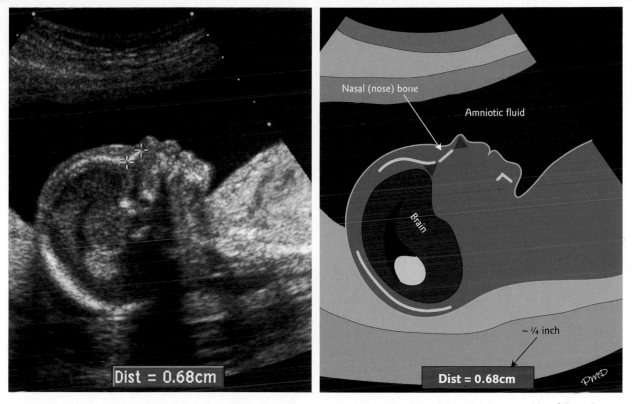

Nasal (nose) bone

Amniotic fluid

Brain

~ ¼ inch

Dist = 0.68cm

Dist = 0.68cm

Nasal (nose) bone

In this nineteen-week baby, the nasal bone is approximately one-quarter of an inch long.

We have now come to the end of our journey through the second and third trimesters. In the remainder of the book, we will take a look at multiple pregnancies: twins, triplets, and more. We will talk about support systems that ensure the health of the baby and give doctors important information about the pregnancy. We also include a few stories—typical of the patients we see—of how doctors use ultrasound to treat pregnancy problems. And finally, we come to the end of our journey with the joyous experience of birth.

Multiple Pregnancies: Twins, Triplets, and Beyond

10

Double Delight: Twins

People are fascinated by the idea of twins, especially if they are identical. Nature replicating itself in this way seems unusual, yet it is not really such an uncommon phenomenon: approximately one pregnant woman out of ninety in the United States gives birth to twins.

There are two types of twins: fraternal and identical. *Fraternal twins* are separate right from the beginning, occurring when two eggs are released by the ovary and each is fertilized by a different sperm. These two fertilized eggs (zygotes) have different chromosomal makeups, and hence the babies are different genetically. So despite the fact that fraternal twins share space inside the uterus, they are no more alike than any other pair of siblings that come from the same parents. (One can be a boy and one a girl, for example.) Since the Greek prefix for two is *di-* and fraternal twins arise from two zygotes, fraternal twins are known in medical terminology as *dizygotic twins*.

Identical twins arise from a single sperm-egg pair, and thus a single zygote (so the medical terminology is *monozygotic twins*). Within a few days after fertilization the group of dividing cells splits into two parts—each with the same genetic makeup, which will result in two identical babies. In the United States, fraternal twins are a little more than twice as common as identical twins.

The pair of diagrams below illustrate the difference between how fraternal (dizygotic) and identical (monozygotic) twins arise.

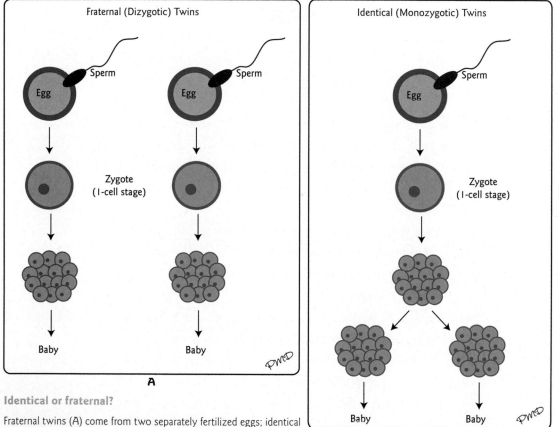

Identical or fraternal?

Fraternal twins (A) come from two separately fertilized eggs; identical twins (B) come from the same fertilized egg that splits into two groups of identical cells within a few days after fertilization.

Degrees of Togetherness

There is more to being twins than sharing or not sharing an egg. Twins also vary in how they share the amnion and chorion that surround them and the placenta that nourishes them. As you may remember from the chapter on the early first trimester, fertilization occurs as the egg travels through the fallopian tube on the way to the uterus, a journey of three to four days. The degree to which twins share the amnion, chorion, and placenta depends on whether they are fraternal or identical twins and, if they are identical, whether the split occurs before or after they reach the uterus (you can look back at the gestational sac diagram in Chapter 1, page 5, to see where the amnion, chorion, and placenta lie in relation to the baby).

Total Separation: Di-Di

If there are two fertilized eggs (fraternal twins), or if a single fertilized egg splits in two (identical twins) *before* it reaches the uterus, each twin will have its own amnion, chorion, and placenta. This situation is called *dichorionic-diamniotic* (*di-di*) and is shown in the diagram on the next page. All fraternal twins, and about one-third of identical twins, are di-di. In the diagram you can see that the separating membrane between di-di twins has four layers—two amnion layers and two chorion layers—and that each twin has its own placenta.

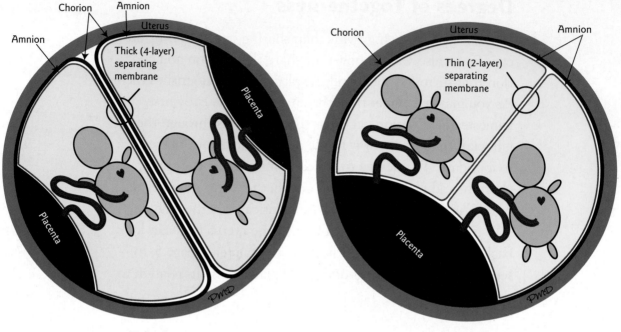

Di-di twins

Mono-di twins

Partial Separation: Mono-Di

Sometimes, twins will share a chorion but have separate amnions. This is called *monochorionic-diamniotic* (*mono-di*). Because these twins share the chorion, they also share the placenta, as you can see in the diagram above, although they are still kept apart by a two-layer separating membrane consisting of both amnions; this is thinner than the four-layer membrane separating di-di twins. Approximately two-thirds of identical twins have this mono-di pattern, which develops when the fertilized group of cells splits after it has already arrived in the uterus, between four and eight days after conception.

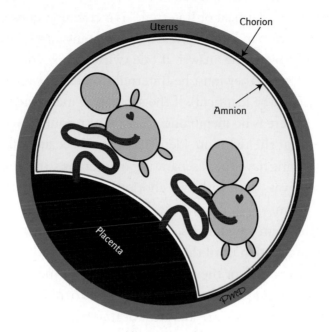

Mono-mono twins

Total Togetherness: Mono-Mono

In rare situations, identical twins share both chorion and amnion. This pattern is called *monochorionic-monoamniotic*, or *mono-mono*. As you can see in the diagram above, no membrane separates such twins as they float around in the amniotic fluid. Each twin has his own umbilical cord, but they share the same placenta. This pattern happens when the split occurs more than eight days after fertilization.

Ultrasound as Twin Detective

"Are my twins identical or fraternal?" is a common question when the ultrasound first shows twins. In many cases, ultrasound can provide the answer. If one twin is a boy and the other a girl, then they must be fraternal (since a boy and a girl obviously can't be identical). If the separating membrane is very thin, or if there is no membrane at all on ultrasound, we can conclude that the twins are identical. This is because all fraternal twins have thick separating membranes, since such twins are always di-di with two chorions and two amnions between them.

In other twin pregnancies, our detective work cannot answer the question until the babies are born. If both babies are of the same sex, or the sex of one or both cannot be seen, and the separating membrane is thick, then there is no way of knowing whether they are identical or fraternal until they make their first appearance!

Views of Identical Twins

The series of images on the following two pages shows identical twins of increasing gestational age. We know these are identical because either they have no membrane between them or a thin, wispy separating membrane.

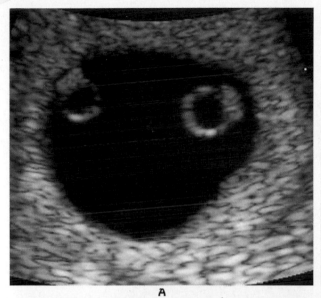

A

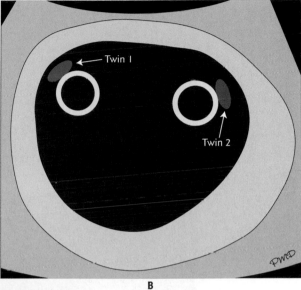

B

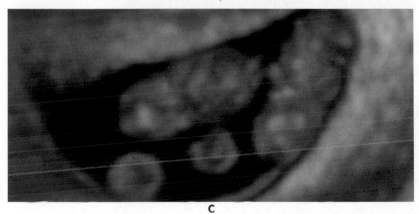

C

Identical twins

At six weeks (A–B); nine weeks (C); ten weeks (D–E); twelve weeks (F–G); and nineteen weeks (H–I). The last pair of twins are of the rare mono-mono variety; the Doppler ultrasound shows blood flowing in their respective umbilical cords, making it clear that the cords are touching each other, meaning that the twins lie within the same amniotic sac.

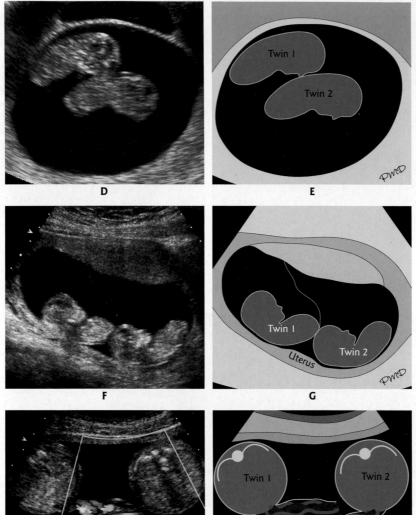

D

E

F

G

H

I

Views of Fraternal Twins

The group of images below leaves no doubt that these eighteen-week twins are fraternal; A and B unmistakably show a boy, while C and D definitely show a girl.

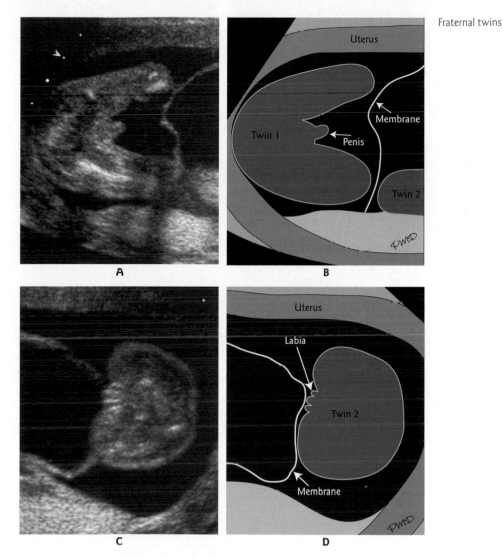

Fraternal twins

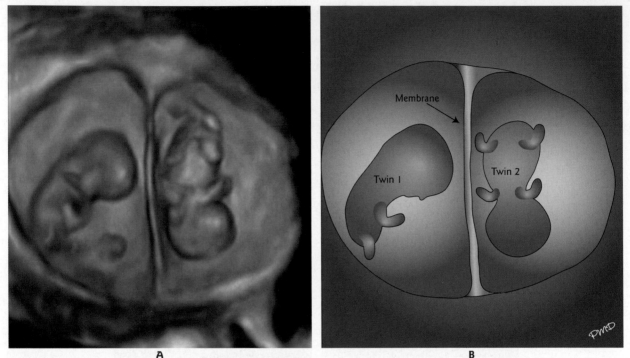

A B

All of the twins in these images can be either fraternal or identical

Ten weeks (A–B); eleven weeks (C–D); seventeen weeks (E–F).

But Sometimes We Can't Be Sure!

The images on this page and the next show twins that could be either identical or fraternal. When twins have a thick membrane between them and are of the same sex or the sex cannot be seen, there is no way of knowing by ultrasound whether they are identical or fraternal. We'll just have to wait until they are born to find out!

Now that we have explored the delights of twins, let's go on to learn about triplets and beyond!

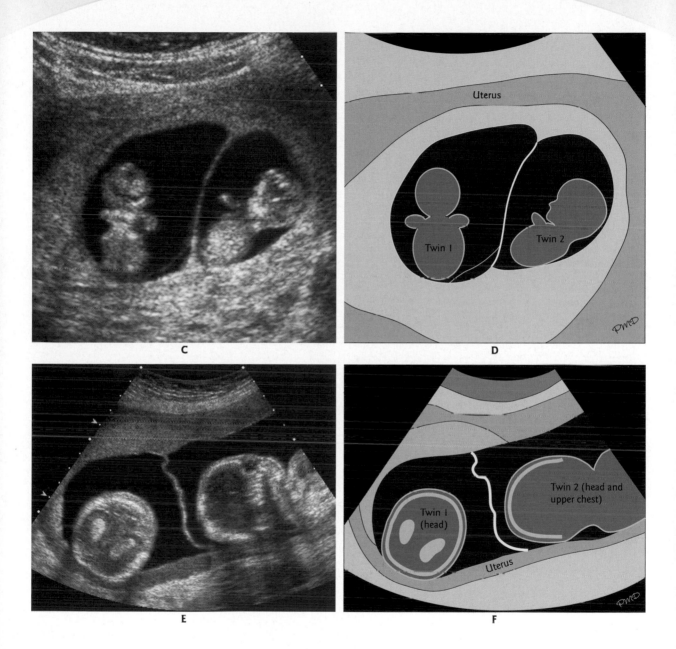

C

D

Uterus

Twin 1

Twin 2

PMcD

E

F

Twin 1 (head)

Twin 2 (head and upper chest)

Uterus

PMcD

11

Triplets and More: Higher-Order Multiple Pregnancies

In 1934, five identical baby girls were born from a single fertilized egg to a Canadian couple in rural Ontario. The odds of such a large multiple birth have been estimated to be about one in sixty-five million, and these babies—the Dionne quintuplets—became an international media sensation. Together they weighed less than fourteen pounds, and each newborn could fit into the palm of an adult hand. They were not expected to survive, but they did, growing into adulthood and eventually writing abut their experiences of being exploited as a tourist attraction in Canada.

Today, with the increasing use of fertility drugs, multiple births are much more common than they used to be. In fact, when women are pregnant with triplets or more, it is almost always the result of fertility treatments. This is because fertility drugs stimulate the ovaries to produce more than one egg, in

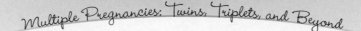

the hopes that at least one will result in a pregnancy, whether by intrauterine insemination or in vitro fertilization.

The explanation of fraternal and identical twins in the previous chapter—along with the variations in shared or multiple placentas and the structure of the membranes separating the babies—apply to higher-order multiple pregnancies as well. Triplets, quadruplets, and higher-order multiples can come in any combination of fraternal and identical groupings. Unlike the identical Dionne quintuplets, higher-order multiple pregnancies that arise from fertility treatments are most often not identical to each other but rather are fraternal. However, it is also possible to have, for example, two identical twins and two fraternal twins in the same pregnancy.

So, without further ado, let's look at some 2D and 3D images of multiple pregnancies.

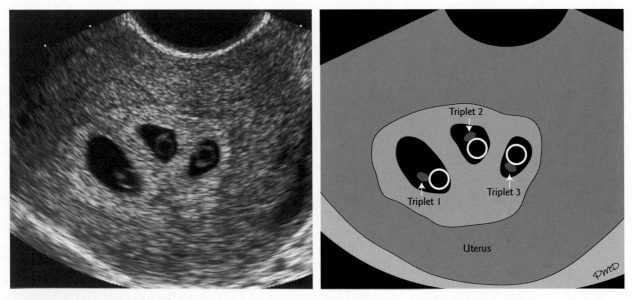

Six-week triplets

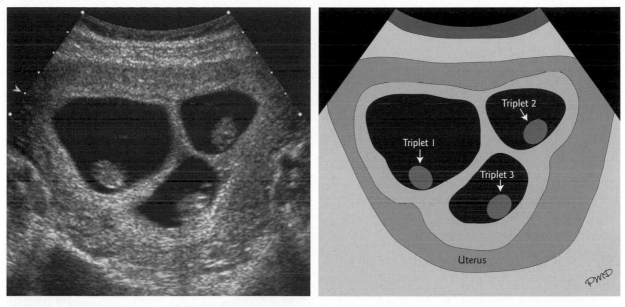

Eight-week triplets

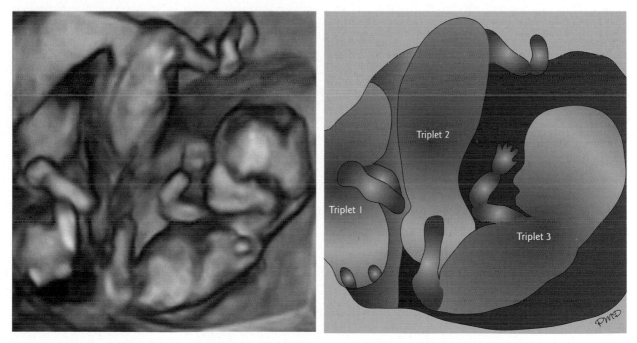

Thirteen-week triplets

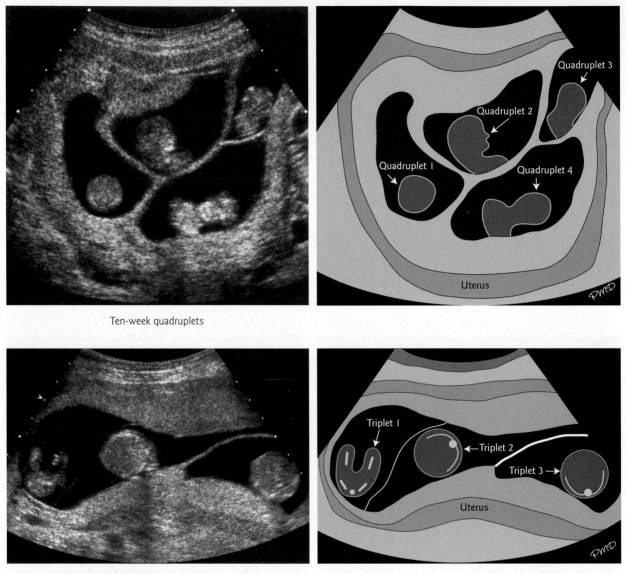

Ten-week quadruplets

Thirteen-week triplets

The pair on the left—triplets 1 and 2—are separated by a thin membrane and therefore are identical. The triplet on the right (triplet 3) is separated from the other two by a thick membrane and so could be identical or fraternal in relation to the other two.

Healthy Mother, Healthy Baby

12

Baby's Caretakers: Placenta, Cord, Amniotic Fluid

The baby has two faithful traveling companions during pregnancy: the placenta and the umbilical cord. Together, they all live within a third vital pregnancy partner, the amniotic fluid. In this chapter we explore these three important pregnancy support systems and show how they nourish and protect the growing baby. In the next chapter we show you how they can give doctors detailed information about the growing baby and even make it possible to treat problems while the baby is still in the uterus.

Dynamic Duo:
Umbilical Cord and Placenta

Caring for the baby

The blood vessels of mother and baby are so close together in the placenta that molecules can transfer back and forth without the two blood systems ever mixing together.

It floats next to the baby, drapes over a shoulder, rests on a thigh, or is held in a tiny hand. The ubiquitous umbilical cord has already appeared in several of the images in this book. It connects the baby to the placenta, and together they provide the baby with nourishment and oxygen from the mother's body. The illustration below shows that one end of the umbilical cord inserts into the baby's body at the front of the abdomen and the other end is attached to the placenta, which has a dual system of blood vessels: one that comes from the mother and the other from the baby.

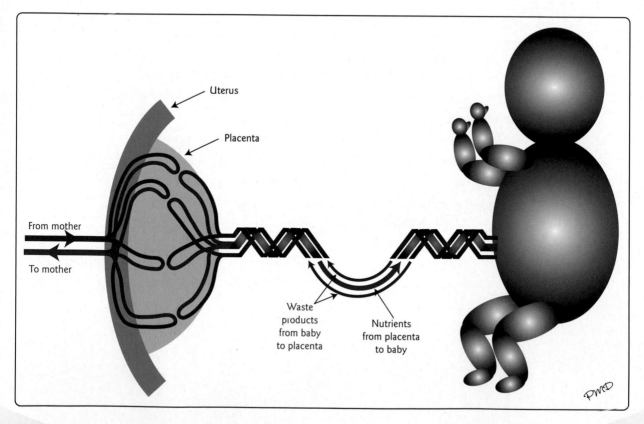

Uterus

Placenta

From mother

To mother

Waste products from baby to placenta

Nutrients from placenta to baby

The umbilical cord contains two umbilical arteries and one umbilical vein. The two arteries travel in parallel, bringing blood filled with waste products and carbon dioxide from the baby to the placenta, their cargo of blood propelled with every beat of the baby's heart. When the baby's blood reaches the placenta, it releases its burdens of waste and carbon dioxide—which are disposed of in the mother's body—and collects fresh oxygen and nutrients from the mother's bloodstream. The umbilical vein then carries this replenished blood back through the umbilical cord to the growing baby. So even before the baby is born, the mother is caring for her child via the umbilical cord and placenta, and she can do this while at work or at a movie—no need for a babysitter yet!

The Placenta: Made-to-Order Nourishment

The placenta contains tissue from both the mother and the baby: decidua from the mother and chorion from the baby (you may remember these terms from earlier chapters). In the early first trimester, these two tissues form a uniform band around the gestational sac. During the middle to late part of the first trimester, part of this band (the part that will become the placenta) persists and thickens, while the rest becomes thinner. By the early second trimester, the thick and thin areas are clearly distinct: the thick area that contains cells from both the baby and mother is the placenta, as seen in the ultrasound and diagram on the next page, while the thin area is the chorionic membrane. The chorionic membrane is not visible on ultrasound, since it is thin and blends in with the uterus, but it is still doing its job surrounding and supporting the baby, umbilical cord, and amniotic fluid.

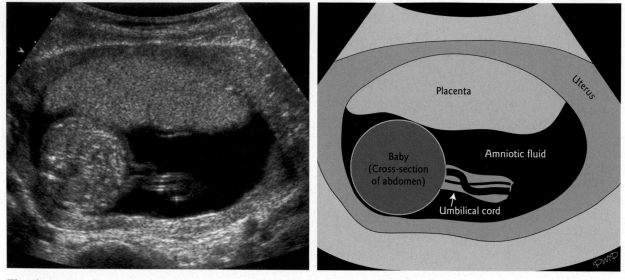

The placenta

In this twenty-week pregnancy the placenta is seen as a thick white structure at the top of the gestational sac.

The placenta can be located just about anywhere in the uterus: bottom, top, front, back, right side, left side. It can be in a different location in every pregnancy. It can even gradually move during the same pregnancy as the uterus grows. The good news is that the placenta can perform its caretaker functions regardless of its location, and that in most cases, the location of the placenta is unimportant. One exception is when the placenta lies low in the uterus, covering the cervix. This condition is called *placenta previa*, as shown on the facing page, and it may make it necessary to deliver the baby by a cesarean section, since the placenta blocks the baby's exit to the birth canal.

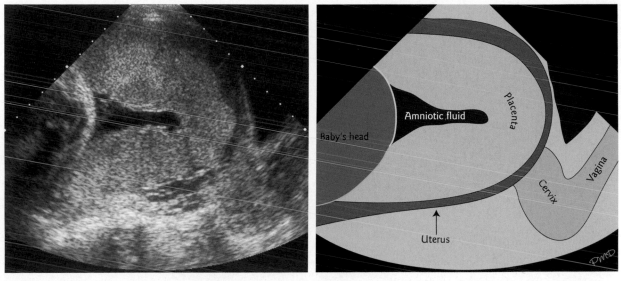

Placenta

Amniotic fluid

Baby's head

Vagina

Cervix

Uterus

Placenta previa

The placenta is located low in the uterus, covering the cervix.

The Umbilical Cord: Baby's Lifeline

The umbilical cord is essential to the baby during pregnancy, but the only vestige of it after birth is the belly button. This is the point at which the umbilical cord emerged from the baby, as seen in the 3D image and diagram on the next page, before detaching from the baby shortly after birth.

As the baby's lifeline, the umbilical cord must be sturdy, and indeed it is. About one and a half feet long and a little less than an inch in diameter, the cord is encased by a strong membrane. The three blood vessels are coiled around each other within the cord and are cushioned by a thick gel called *Wharton's jelly*. This is a protective arrangement, since it allows the cord to bend, turn around, and even be kicked against the uterine wall by an exuberant foot without any interruption to the smooth flow of blood within it. The strong membrane and thick jelly, as well as the flexible, coiled vessels themselves, all prevent any ruptures or kinks that could impede blood flow. You can get a view of the coiling of the blood vessels in the

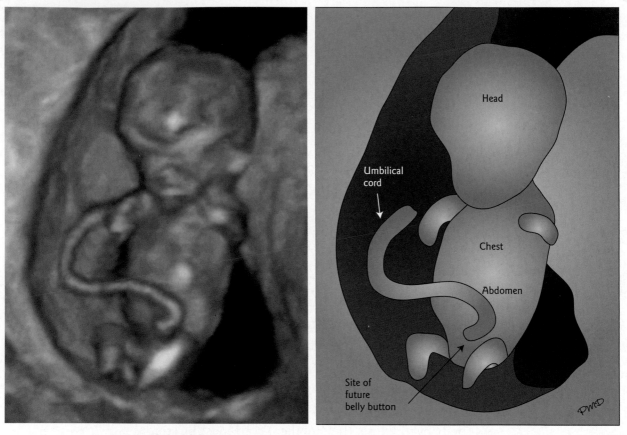

Labels on illustration: Head, Umbilical cord, Chest, Abdomen, Site of future belly button

A view of the lifeline

The umbilical cord is seen coming out of this eighteen-week baby's abdomen on a 3D ultrasound.

umbilical cord on the 2D image on the opposite page, which shows the interior of the cord.

The blood vessels of the umbilical cord insert into the placenta, as you can see in the color Doppler image on the opposite page. The point of insertion is usually in the middle of the placenta, which gives the blood vessels plenty of room to branch off in all directions, releasing the baby's waste and carbon dioxide and picking up oxygen and nutrients from the mother.

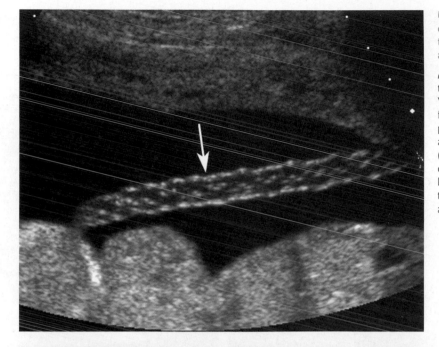

Umbilical cord traveling through the amniotic fluid

An arrow points to the umbilical cord. While the cord follows a straight path through the amniotic fluid (which appears black on ultrasound), the blood vessels within the cord are curled and coiled inside.

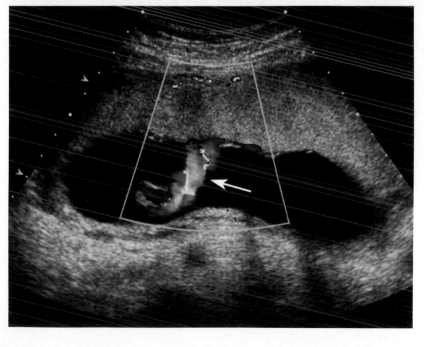

Point of contact

This color Doppler image shows blood flowing in the umbilical cord (denoted by an arrow) where it attaches to the placenta. The placenta is on the front wall of the uterus.

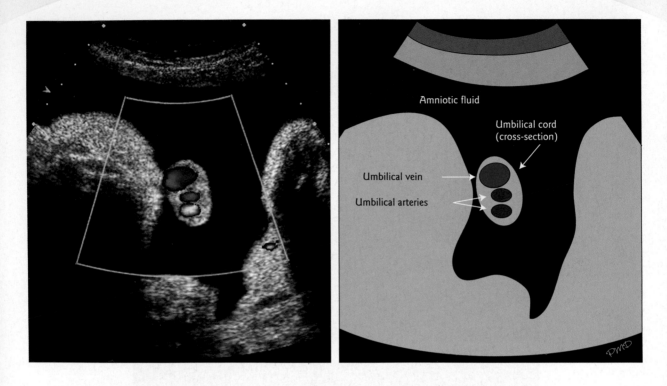

Our final views of the umbilical cord show the movement of blood in the umbilical arteries and veins as seen on Doppler ultrasounds. The image above demonstrates the flow of blood in the two arteries as red-orange and the flow of blood in the vein as blue.

Spectral Doppler ultrasound, which measures and shows how fast the blood is flowing in a vessel over time, makes the image on the next page possible. The top of the image is a 2D view of the umbilical artery. The bottom is a Doppler waveform showing how fast the blood is moving in one part of the umbilical artery—the part between the two short lines (the Doppler gate). The peaks of the Doppler waveform show the speed during each of the baby's heartbeats, when blood is flowing the fastest in the umbilical arteries, and the troughs show the

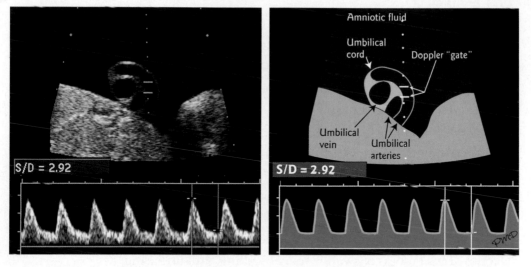

Vibrant velocity

These spectral Doppler ultrasounds measure how quickly blood is flowing in the umbilical artery.

Labels on figure: Amniotic fluid; Umbilical cord; Doppler "gate"; Umbilical vein; Umbilical arteries; S/D = 2.92; S/D = 2.92

slower speed between heartbeats. The ratio of the fastest flow (S) to the slowest flow (D) during the cardiac cycle is used to check on the baby's health. In this baby the ratio (S/D) is normal at 2.92.

Baby's Protector: The Amniotic Fluid

One of the most dramatic moments of pregnancy is when the mother's "water breaks." What is the purpose of this "water," where does it come from, and how much of it is there?

The amniotic fluid is the baby's protector: It cushions the baby and absorbs impacts that might otherwise cause injury—for example, if the mother bumps into something with that growing abdomen, or if she lies on her belly. It also allows for unrestricted growth of the baby's body, including the muscles, bones, and joints of the arms and legs, as well as the chest and lungs. The fluid also insulates the baby—keeping the baby's temperature normal inside the uterus, no matter how cold or hot the mother is outside!

Fluid Dynamics

In the first trimester, the amniotic fluid comes from molecules that seep (by a process called *diffusion*) into the gestational sac from the mother's body. As the baby develops through the first trimester, the mother's body expertly keeps the right amount of amniotic fluid in the gestational sac.

In the second and third trimesters, the baby's urine becomes the main source of amniotic fluid. (We saw ultrasound images of baby urination in Chapter 8.) The baby not only produces its own amniotic fluid, but also swallows fluid, which is then absorbed into its bloodstream. Some of this fluid is passed back to the mother through the umbilical cord to the placenta. This process of swallowing, absorbing, and urinating amniotic fluid keeps the correct balance of fluid inside the sac.

From an Ounce to a Quart

So how much fluid is there? At ten weeks, the sac contains about one fluid ounce of amniotic fluid; at twenty weeks there is about a pint. The amount of fluid peaks at thirty-seven weeks, when the baby is surrounded by between one and a half and two pints of fluid. There is a slight decrease in the amount of fluid after this point.

Fill 'er Up

During the first trimester, amniotic fluid does not fill the entire gestational sac, as you can see in the ultrasound and illustration on the opposite page. At this stage, the amnion (the thin inner membrane) is separate from the chorion (the membrane that forms the outer lining of the gestational sac). The fluid within the gestational sac includes both amniotic fluid—the fluid inside the amnion—as well as chorionic fluid (the fluid between the amnion and chorion).

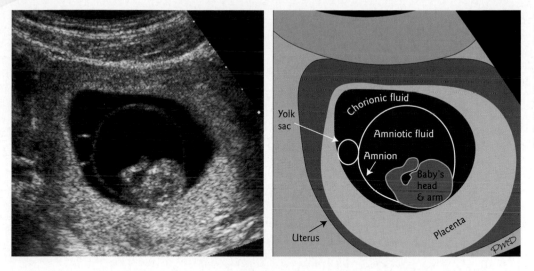

Amniotic fluid in the first trimester

Notice how there is fluid both inside and around the amnion (the thin internal membrane) in this eleven-week pregnancy.

As the first trimester progresses, the amnion gradually expands until it reaches the periphery of the gestational sac by the early second trimester. From that point onward, all of the fluid surrounding the baby is amniotic fluid.

Now that we have learned about the nourishing and protective functions of the baby's support systems, it is time to understand their usefulness as sources of medical information about the pregnancy and the baby.

13

Tests for the Baby's Health: Amniocentesis and Others

Ultrasound lets the doctor check on some aspects of the baby's health, especially those that involve the baby's structure and size. There are other tests that can be used together with ultrasound to get extra information about the baby. Some of these tests involve the pregnancy support systems that we discussed in the previous chapter: *amniocentesis*, which removes amniotic fluid for testing; *chorionic villus sampling* (CVS), which obtains small pieces of the placenta for evaluation; and *umbilical blood sampling*, which involves removing a sample of the baby's blood to be analyzed. The most frequently used of these procedures is amniocentesis. These tests are performed only if there are certain indications that the baby might be at risk and that the test can provide the doctor with information to help care for the mother and baby. Such indications include the age of the mother (thirty-five or older), a family history of or a previous child with hereditary disease, or an ultrasound finding that raises concern for the health of the baby.

Amniocentesis

Amniocentesis is the removal of a sample of amniotic fluid from the gestational sac through a thin needle. This test can be used to check for hereditary or genetic diseases—such as Down syndrome, an abnormality of the baby's chromosomes—that may not show up on ultrasound alone. It also has other uses in special circumstances, such as to check for infection in the amniotic fluid that might require treatment, or to determine whether the baby's lungs are ready to work on their own to breathe air.

You might wonder how the fluid that the baby is floating in can give us information about the baby's chromosomes. The answer lies in the behavior of cells. Every time you touch or brush your skin against something, some of your skin cells fall off. These cells are microscopic, of course, so you don't see them. The same thing happens to the baby. Even though the baby is floating in amniotic fluid, skin cells are always falling off and floating around in the fluid. By removing a small amount of amniotic fluid, we get a sample of the baby's cells and put these cells through a genetic analysis to find out about the baby's chromosomal and genetic makeup.

Amniocentesis is not a new procedure; it has been used for about fifty years, well before the common use of ultrasound. But today, thanks to ultrasound, amniocentesis is safer than ever. As you can see in the diagram on the facing page, a needle is inserted into the gestational sac and a syringe is used to withdraw a small amount of fluid—about four teaspoons for a genetic diagnosis, and considerably less for other testing. Because the baby is moving around in that same fluid, continuous ultrasound guidance is used to make sure that the needle does not poke the baby. If the baby approaches the needle, this will be seen on the ultrasound image and the doctor can move the needle away from the baby.

During this relatively painless procedure, about one-half to one and a half inches of the needle extends into the amniotic fluid, which is then drawn up into a syringe. When the right amount of fluid has been withdrawn, the needle is removed, and the uterine wall closes up tightly over the tiny hole so that there is no bleeding or leakage of fluid.

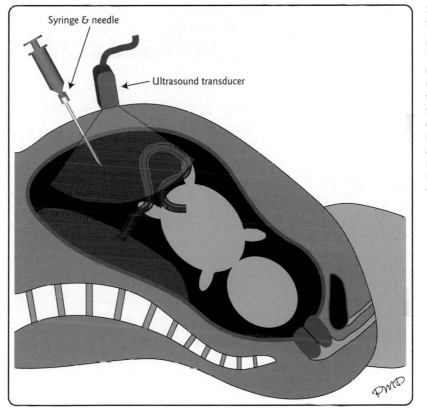

Syringe & needle

Ultrasound transducer

Stay away from that baby!

Under the watchful "eye" of the ultrasound image (the gray area under the ultrasound transducer in the diagram), the doctor makes sure that the amniocentesis needle stays away from the baby and the umbilical cord.

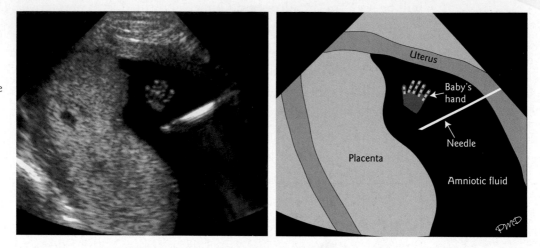

Amniocentesis in a sixteen-week pregnancy

Ultrasound monitoring helps the doctor make sure the needle avoids the baby.

The ultrasound image above shows you what the doctor sees on the ultrasound screen when performing an amniocentesis, along with a helpful illustration.

Chorionic Villus Sampling

Chorionic villus sampling, commonly referred to as CVS, is another way to test for certain hereditary or genetic abnormalities when there are indications that the baby might be at risk. It is important to realize that even if a doctor recommends a CVS or amniocentesis, in the vast majority of cases the results of these tests turn out to be normal and the baby is healthy.

When there are indications for an amniocentesis or CVS for genetic testing, how do the doctor and mother choose between these two tests? Amniocentesis, a quicker and simpler procedure than CVS, is chosen more often than CVS. But CVS provides answers at an earlier point in pregnancy than amniocentesis. CVS is usually done between ten and twelve weeks' gestation, and the results are available in just a few days, while amniocentesis is commonly done at fifteen to eighteen weeks' gestation, and the results come back one to two weeks later. So CVS is often chosen if the mother or doctor doesn't want to wait until after fifteen weeks to get the answer.

A Genetic Blueprint

As we learned in earlier chapters, the placenta is made up of cells that come from both mother and baby. The chorion is the part of the placenta that comes from the baby, so its cells have the same genetic makeup as the baby. By extracting some cells—called *chorionic villi* (plural of *villus*)—from the placenta, growing them in the laboratory, and looking at their chromosomes, we can see a genetic blueprint of the baby and determine whether there are genetic abnormalities. There are two ways to remove the chorionic villus cells, each shown in the diagrams below.

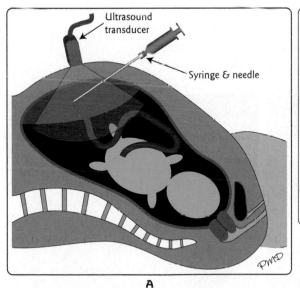

A

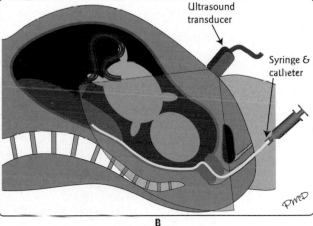

B

Chorionic villus sampling

The shaded areas below the ultrasound transducer on the diagrams show the region seen in the ultrasound image. The transabdominal approach (A) uses a needle inserted through the mother's abdomen and the wall of the uterus into the placenta. The transcervical approach (B) uses a flexible catheter inserted through the mother's vagina and cervix, with the tip advanced into the placenta.

Transabdominal CVS. This method involves inserting a needle through the mother's abdomen into the placenta (A), guided by ultrasound. Once the needle is in the proper location, tiny pieces of placenta are removed by the suction of a syringe attached to the needle.

Transcervical CVS. This method uses a soft catheter inserted into the vagina and through the cervix, and then threaded—using ultrasound guidance—along the outside of the gestational sac until the tip is inserted into the placenta (B). Then small bits of placenta are drawn out into the syringe.

Following either CVS procedure, a technician takes the contents of the syringe and uses a special technique to separate the baby's cells (chorionic villi) from the mother's cells (decidua). The baby's cells are then genetically analyzed.

The decision about whether to use the transabdominal or transcervical technique depends, in part, on the location of the placenta. If the placenta is in the front of the uterus, a

Transabdominal chorionic villus sampling in a twelve-week pregnancy

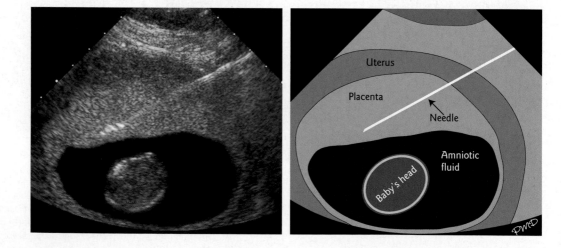

transabdominal CVS is generally best; if it is toward the mother's back, the transcervical technique is often used. Whichever technique is chosen, the test is relatively painless for the mother and the needle or catheter does not enter the gestational sac or touch the baby.

Chorionic Villus Sampling in Real Life

The ultrasound images and accompanying diagrams show you what the doctor inserting the needle or catheter sees on the ultrasound screen when performing chorionic villus sampling. The image on the preceding page shows a transabdominal CVS. You can see the needle as a straight white line ending up in the placenta. Ultrasound guidance makes sure that the needle is in the placenta and does not enter into the amniotic fluid or come into contact with the baby. The image below shows the insertion of a catheter—seen as a curved white line—for a transcervical CVS, again using ultrasound guidance to make sure that the procedure is safe and successful.

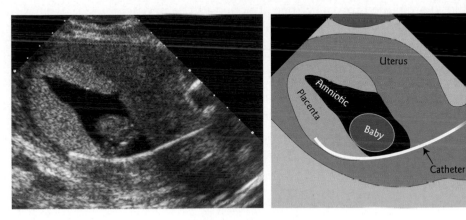

Transcervical chorionic villus sampling in a twelve-week pregnancy

Umbilical Blood Sampling

Doctors often use blood tests to check on the health of a patient. An obstetrician caring for a pregnant woman will often do blood tests on the mother, such as a test in early pregnancy to confirm that she is in fact pregnant, or a test for blood sugar levels to check for diabetes. Occasionally, the obstetrician needs to examine the baby's blood to make sure that the baby is healthy. This might be done to check whether the baby is anemic or to test for the presence of enzymes in the baby's blood that might indicate a health concern.

When the doctor needs to do a blood test on the baby, blood is obtained from the umbilical vein—which is located inside the umbilical cord and transports blood from the placenta to the baby. Using ultrasound guidance, a tiny needle is passed through the mother's abdomen into the point at which the umbilical cord attaches to the placenta. This is a good spot because the cord is anchored there and does not move. A few drops of blood are pulled into a syringe attached to the needle. There is no pain to the baby and very little to the mother, since the placenta and umbilical cord do not have nerves to feel pain.

In rare circumstances, a similar procedure can be done to treat the baby when a problem is present. For example, if the baby is anemic the doctor can give the baby a transfusion by injecting blood into the umbilical vein. In other cases, medication can be injected.

The drawings on the next page show the positions of the ultrasound transducer, needle, syringe, and umbilical cord when umbilical blood sampling is done. The path of the needle depends on where the placenta is located and where the umbilical cord attaches to it. If the placenta is in the front of

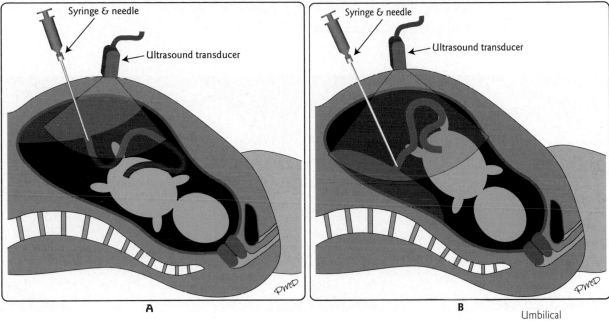

Syringe & needle

Ultrasound transducer

Syringe & needle

Ultrasound transducer

A

B

Umbilical
blood sampling

the uterus (A), the needle goes through the placenta into the umbilical vein without going through the amniotic fluid. If the placenta is in the back, toward the mother's spine (B), the needle must go through the amniotic fluid to get to the umbilical vein. During these procedures, the doctor uses ultrasound to guide the needle into the proper location and to avoid any contact with the baby. Whether the placenta is in the front or the back, the needle enters the umbilical cord where it is anchored to the placenta.

The images and diagrams below show the umbilical blood sampling procedure in real life, with the placenta in different locations.

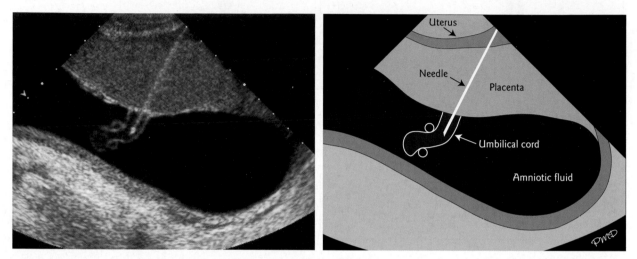

Umbilical blood sampling when the placenta is in the front of the uterus

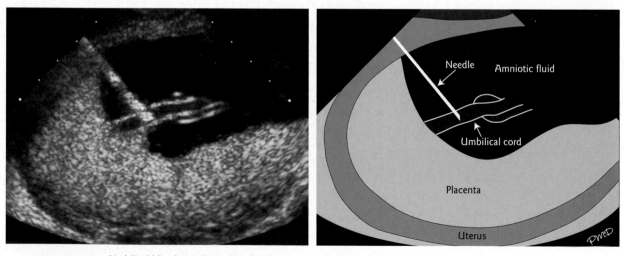

Umbilical blood sampling when the placenta is in the back of the uterus

14

Preventing Problems: Knowledge Is Power

In the vast majority of cases, pregnancies proceed smoothly and result in healthy babies. Sometimes, however, there may be problems with the baby's development. But thanks to the technology of ultrasound and advances in medical treatment, many of these problems can be treated and eliminated. In this chapter, we share several stories drawn from our experiences with these kinds of pregnancy problems. (In order to protect our patients' privacy, these are not stories of actual patients but rather fictionalized accounts.)

In most of these stories, an ultrasound scan alerted us to a problem in time to schedule treatments that ensured the continued good health of the mother and baby. In one story, ultrasound combined with amniocentesis detected the absence of a genetic disease, which provided happy reassurance to the expectant parents for the remainder of the pregnancy.

All of these stories share one common experience: the power of knowledge. The more doctors know about the pregnancy and the baby growing inside the uterus, the better able they are to intervene if necessary to ensure the birth of healthy babies.

Creating a Family[1]

Caroline and Don married in their late twenties and had planned to have their first child within a few years. "We had it all figured out," says Caroline, an architect. "I would be far enough along in my career to take a leave from my job and try to work at home." But when they were ready for parenthood, Nature had other ideas. After nearly two years of trying without success to get pregnant, Caroline and Don were deeply discouraged. "We didn't want to give up, however," says Don. "So we decided to go to a fertility clinic."

At the clinic, Caroline was diagnosed as having blocked fallopian tubes, a condition that was preventing her from becoming pregnant. After discussing the options with their doctor, the couple decided to try *in vitro* fertilization (IVF). Caroline was given medication that would stimulate her ovaries to produce more eggs. Every other day for two weeks, early each morning she went to the clinic for ultrasounds. This allowed the doctor to see how her ovaries were responding to the medication. "A bit of an inconvenience, but worth it if it meant we could get pregnant," remembers Caroline.

---

1. For more information about preparing for pregnancy, please see Chapter 2.

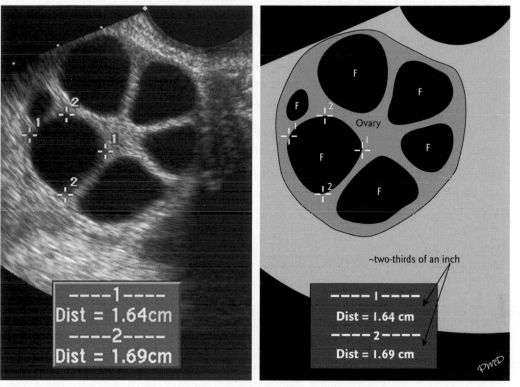

A plethora of large follicles

One of the follicles (F) is being measured here.

Labels on diagram: F, F, F, F, F, F, Ovary, ~two-thirds of an inch

---1----
Dist = 1.64cm
----2----
Dist = 1.69cm

---- 1 ----
Dist = 1.64 cm
---- 2 ----
Dist = 1.69 cm

The ultrasound and its accompanying diagram above show what Caroline's ovary looked like on the tenth day. Instead of just one dominant follicle, which is what normally happens, her ovary has several large follicles. We know that most of the follicles contain eggs, but they are too small to see. Six follicles are seen on this one image, but she had a total of fourteen follicles in both of her ovaries.

When the doctor determined that the time was right, the eggs were removed from her ovary during a procedure monitored by ultrasound and mixed with Don's sperm in a test tube. The next day, seven eggs had successfully fertilized, on their way to becoming embryos. A couple of days later, three of the embryos were put into Caroline's uterus and the other four were frozen for future attempts at pregnancy. "Then we had to wait to see if I became pregnant," says Caroline. "We were so nervous, but hopeful, too." Four weeks later, Caroline returned to the clinic for an ultrasound and received wonderful news. "Two of them took," says Don. "Caroline was pregnant with twins! We saw two sacs and two tiny heartbeats flickering on the screen. It was absolutely thrilling after all this time." The twins would, of course, be fraternal, rather than identical, since each came from a different fertilized egg.

Caroline's pregnancy was uneventful, except that the couple had to buy two of everything to get ready for their babies! You can see the twins on a 3D ultrasound and diagram below at ten weeks, each floating around in a separate gestational sac. Here, as you can see, one twin prefers being upside down!

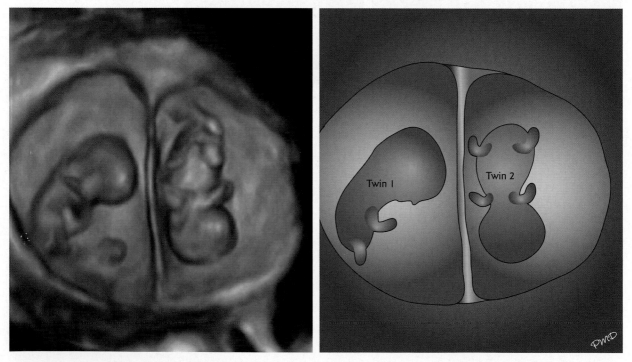

Ten-week twins after fertility treatment

After several more months of eager anticipation, Caroline and Don became the proud parents of a healthy boy and girl. "They are now three years old and the best of friends," says Caroline. "I guess they got used to being together all the time!"

Saving a Life[2]

Gabriela was twenty-six years old and happily married, had a great job, and—she thought—had no worries. "I even thought I might be pregnant," she says. "We had done a test at home that was positive. This was great, because we had been hoping to have a child." But one day, a nagging pain in her right side prompted her to call her doctor. "Something just didn't feel right," she explains. That call saved her life. The doctor ordered an ultrasound that revealed an *ectopic* pregnancy— which means a pregnancy in the wrong place. She did have a fertilized egg, but it had implanted outside of her uterus. This kind of pregnancy can never result in a baby, since it cannot receive adequate nourishment or support from the mother. To make matters worse, as the pregnancy increases in size, it can cause bleeding in the mother's pelvis that can be life threatening.

---

2. For more information about the early first trimester of pregnancy, please see Chapter 3.

A dangerous ectopic pregnancy developing outside the uterus

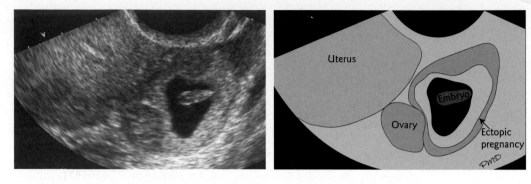

"Once he saw the ultrasound, my doctor did not even let me go home," recalls Gabriela. "He said he had to take immediate action to protect my health." The ultrasound and illustration above show what the doctor was looking at: a pregnancy developing outside of Gabriela's uterus.

The good news is that a few months later, Gabriela became pregnant again. "This time, everything was in the right place," says Gabriela. You can see her six-week embryo below.

Early the following spring, Gabriela delivered a seven-pound little girl. "She's so precious," the new mother bubbles.

A normal pregnancy six months after the ectopic pregnancy was removed

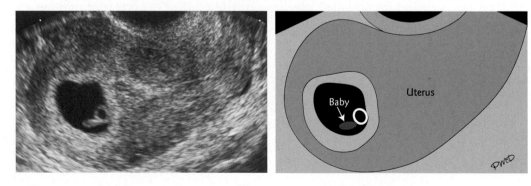

The Heart of the Matter[3]

Liling and Qiang were looking forward confidently to their second baby. Their daughter was three years old and was excited about "the baby growing in Mommy's tummy." But during the nineteenth week of pregnancy, the doctor called them to his office after a routine ultrasound. "Your baby's heart has all of the four chambers," he began, "but we are seeing on ultrasound that the two main blood vessels coming out of the heart are switched. This is no problem during the pregnancy, but will need to be corrected after birth, so I'd like you to see a pediatric cardiologist [a heart expert for children]."

"We were shocked," says Liling. "No one in our family had ever had a heart problem, and we were really worried about the idea of surgery for our baby." But after the visit with the cardiologist, the couple felt somewhat relieved. "He confirmed the diagnosis," says Qiang, "but assured us that putting the blood vessels into their correct locations would repair the heart completely so our baby could live a normal life." The images on the next page show how the blood vessel problem was diagnosed.

---

3. For more information about the heart, please see Chapter 6.

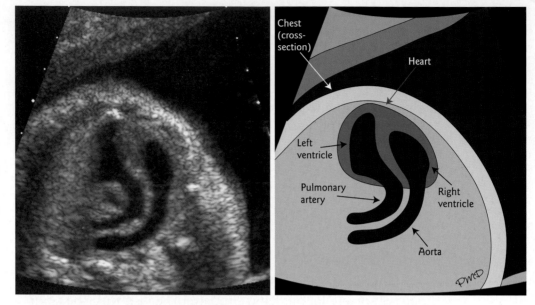

In this baby, the aorta and the pulmonary artery—the two major blood vessels—are coming out of the heart in parallel instead of the normal crisscross pattern. This appearance means that the aorta is attached to the right ventricle and the pulmonary artery to the left ventricle, the reverse of normal.

The rest of Liling's pregnancy was uneventful. "Surgery was scheduled for shortly after our baby was born," said Liling, "and the cardiologist explained to us that the outcome is better when they know about the problem before birth." The surgery was successful, and the couple now has two very active preschoolers. "They keep us running!" says Qiang.

First Alert for Safety[4]

Alessandra and Julio always came to their prenatal visits together. "We wanted to share every bit of the experience of our first child," says Julio. The couple was excited about their routine ultrasound scan at eighteen weeks. They were a bit surprised, though, when the sonographer (ultrasound

---

4. For more information about the kidneys, please see Chapter 6.

technologist) seemed to spend a very long time looking at one part of the scan. "These are your baby's kidneys," she explained. Then she left the room to bring in the doctor, who also looked closely at the screen. "It looks like your baby has a little extra urine in his kidneys," said the doctor. "We see this quite often, especially in boys. It means that the kidneys are not draining the urine into the bladder properly. In most cases, this is nothing serious."

Alessandra and Julio were worried. "We asked the doctor what this meant for our baby," remembers Julio. "Her answer was reassuring. She told us that most of the time the problem corrects itself before birth and all of the urine starts flowing into the bladder correctly. But even if the problem is still there when the baby is born, the ultrasound has alerted us so that it can be treated."

There are black circular areas within each kidney where the urine is collecting. If you compare this image and diagram with the image of normal kidneys in Chapter 6 (page 69), you can see that there is much more urine collecting here than in the normal kidneys.

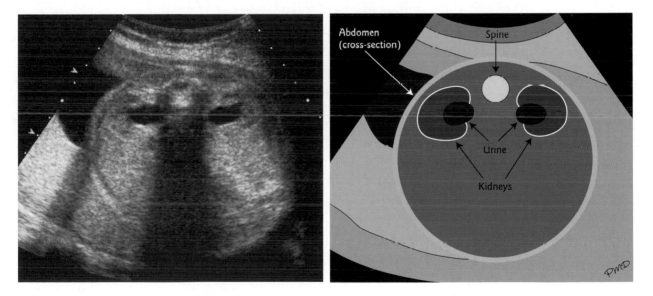

The doctor had the couple come in again at thirty-two weeks for another ultrasound, which showed that the urine was still not draining completely out of the kidneys, as seen on the preceding page. The doctor explained that the baby might have a condition called *reflux*, which means that some of the urine that has flowed down the ureter (the tube connecting the kidneys to the bladder) to the bladder flows back up into the kidneys. "Again, the doctor assured us that normal growth and development either before or after birth often eliminates the problem," said Alessandra. "It was hard to think of our baby having any problem at all, but at least the ultrasound helped us prepare emotionally and alerted the doctors to follow up with treatment."

Little Raul was born a month later, "peeing up a storm," says Alessandra. Two weeks after birth, tests confirmed that the baby did have reflux, so the pediatrician prescribed antibiotics to protect the kidneys. "We were still a bit anxious for a few months," says Julio. "Although he certainly was going through a lot of diapers!" More tests at ten months, however, gave the parents the happy news that the reflux was gone. "Your baby is perfectly fine now," said the pediatrician. "It's lucky we caught the problem before he was born and gave him the antibiotics, because Raul might otherwise have had permanent damage to his kidneys."

What happened to this baby shows how prenatal ultrasound can prevent some forms of serious kidney disease early in life. In fact, now that ultrasound has become routinely used in pregnant women, the rate of childhood kidney failure has been dramatically reduced.

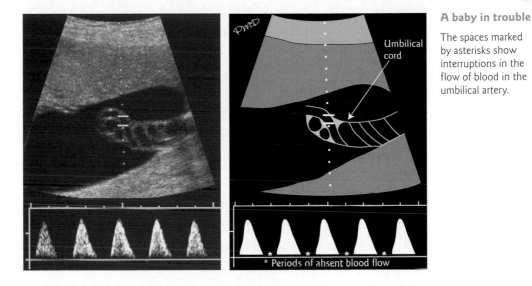

A baby in trouble

The spaces marked by asterisks show interruptions in the flow of blood in the umbilical artery.

Rescuing a Baby in Trouble[5]

Yvonne was in the twenty-eighth week of her pregnancy and going for what she thought would be a routine prenatal visit with her doctor. But this visit turned out differently. "You haven't gained quite as much weight as I would have expected by this time," said the doctor. "Let's get an ultrasound to check on the baby." Yvonne was not concerned at first. "I felt fine and could feel the baby moving," she says, "so I thought my baby was fine, too." However, the ultrasound revealed that the baby was unusually small, which could mean that the placenta was not delivering enough oxygen and other nourishment to meet the baby's needs.

Yvonne's doctor prescribed bed rest and weekly ultrasounds to monitor the health of the baby. Three weeks later, the Doppler ultrasound shown above demonstrated an abnormal

---

5. For more information about umbilical cord blood flow, please see Chapter 12.

waveform in the arteries of the umbilical cord, because blood stopped flowing briefly between each of the baby's heartbeats. This was further evidence of trouble because it meant the placenta was losing ability to supply the baby with adequate oxygen and nutrients. With this change in the umbilical cord blood flow, the doctor scheduled Yvonne to come in twice a week for ultrasounds to keep a close eye on the baby.

One week later, when Yvonne came in for her ultrasound, the situation became even more serious: the Doppler below showed not only interruptions in the flow of blood, but that blood was flowing *backward* in the umbilical arteries between each of the baby's heartbeats. An additional sign of trouble was seen on the ultrasound: the amount of amniotic fluid was now abnormally low. "My doctor explained all of this to me and told me that he needed to do a cesarean section that day to save the baby's life. I was so scared," says Yvonne. "My baby boy was really small when he came out, weighing just under three pounds, and he needed a few weeks in the neonatal intensive care unit before we were allowed to bring him home. Since

The situation worsens

Blood in the umbilical artery not only stops flowing, but actually flows backward, between each of the baby's heartbeats.

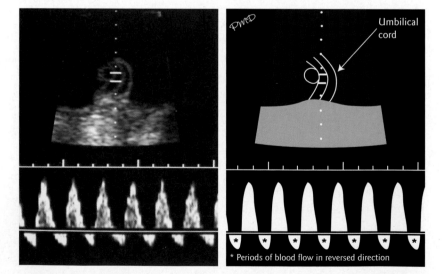

Umbilical cord

* Periods of blood flow in reversed direction

then he hasn't stopped eating! I just don't want to think about what would have happened if the ultrasound had not detected the problem."

Genetic Peace of Mind[6]

After five years of marriage, Rachel and Jonathan were ready to have a child. They were both Jews of eastern European origin—a high-risk group for Tay-Sachs disease, a fatal and incurable condition. So they had blood tests to determine whether they were carriers. "We knew that Tay-Sachs is transmitted by a recessive gene," says Rachel. "So we would both have to be carriers for there to be a potential problem. Unfortunately, both of us carried the deadly gene, meaning that any pregnancy would have a one in four chance of being affected."

Jonathan added, "When Rachel got pregnant a few years ago, we were worried, of course. But our doctor had assured us that she would perform an amniocentesis during the pregnancy to find out whether the baby had Tay-Sachs." Because the amniocentesis was performed during week sixteen of the pregnancy, the usual time for this procedure, Rachel and Jonathan spent an anxious four months, but they were rewarded by the happy news that their baby was free of the disease. "As an added bonus, the ultrasound for the amniocentesis also told us that we were going to have a son," says Jonathan, "so we spent the next five months very relieved, talking over boys' names and decorating the nursery! We're even thinking about Sam's bar mitzvah, but right now he's more interested in Matchbox cars."

---

6. For more information about tests for the baby's health in the uterus, please see Chapter 13.

A Life-Saving Blood Transfusion in the Uterus[7]

The last thing future parents want to think about is harm coming to their unborn baby, but Caitlin and Sean were faced with this reality during their second pregnancy. Because of Rh antibodies in her blood developed during her first pregnancy, Caitlin's immune system was now attacking the red blood cells of her second baby. This was causing the baby's red blood cells to die. "Our doctor told us that we needed to monitor the baby's blood cells closely to see if he was becoming anemic, which could be dangerous," says Caitlin.

So beginning at twenty weeks, Caitlin's doctor performed special Doppler ultrasounds to study the flow of blood to the baby's brain, looking for signs of anemia. "Up until about twenty-four weeks, the blood flow looked normal," says Sean. By the twenty-sixth week of pregnancy, however, the ultrasound showed that the blood flow was getting faster and faster in order to deliver the same amount of oxygen to the brain. This meant that the number of the baby's red blood cells had dropped to dangerously low levels.

An ultrasound-guided umbilical blood sampling test confirmed that the baby was anemic. "Things suddenly started happening very quickly," says Caitlin. "After the baby's blood was tested, the doctor told me they needed to transfuse healthy blood into the baby, because it was too early for a safe delivery."

Guided by the ultrasound image, the doctor maneuvered the tiny transfusion needle into the baby's umbilical vein where it attached to the placenta, sending healthy blood directly into

---

7. For more information about tests and procedures in the uterus, please see Chapter 13.

the baby's bloodstream. This procedure—inserting a needle into a vein that is only two millimeters in diameter—is extremely delicate. "I had to stay very still," says Caitlin. "My husband and I held hands and focused all our thoughts on our baby." The procedure was successful, and the baby's anemia was reversed. After two more transfusions during the pregnancy, Caitlin gave birth to her new son at thirty-three weeks, weighing in at five pounds. "He had another blood transfusion right after birth and a few weeks of special care, and he's been a perfectly healthy little boy since," says Caitlin. "When I look at his bouncing energy now, I often think back to those many ultrasounds I had and the transfusions that saved his life."

The Main Event: Labor and Birth

15

A New Life Begins

The astonishing technology of ultrasound gives us a front-row seat during the developing pregnancy. Not only do we witness the emergence of the baby's face and body, we also examine the delicate and complex structures of the internal organs. And, as the stories in the previous chapter describe, we are able to probe even deeper into the world of the womb to diagnose and treat potential problems before birth.

But of course all of the ultrasound activities during the nine months of pregnancy have only one purpose—the safe entrance into the world of a new, unique human being. Detailed and descriptive as images on a screen may be, they cannot compare to the momentous experience of birth and the sweet reality of holding your newborn baby in your arms. Before that can happen, however, the complicated drama of birth has to unfold, and who better to explain these dramatic details to you than someone who has delivered thousands of babies? So we turned to one of our colleagues, obstetrician Lydia K. Lee, M.D., for help.

In a fortunate coincidence for all, Lydia had just given birth to her own twin boys (by planned cesarean section) as we were completing the manuscript for this book! Fresh from the birth experience, she was only too happy to share both her emotions and her experience delivering babies. (And, as a proud mother, she also shared photos of her newborn sons, Maxwell and Benjamin.)

Dr. Lydia Lee's twin boys, newly in the world

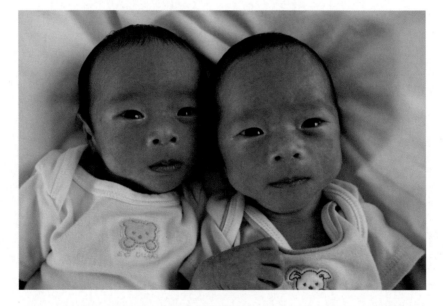

"Experiencing the birth of my own children was like nothing I could have imagined," Lydia says. "Even though I have delivered thousands of babies, to actually see life emerge from my own body, and to hold a baby who was a part of my husband and me, was exhilarating. All of my medical knowledge flew out of my head at that moment, and I was completely and exclusively a mother."

During Lydia's pregnancy, we and the ultrasound staff had all watched these boys as they grew from tiny embryos to the adorable babies you see here. But as radiologists, we are not usually present in the delivery room, so it is always a thrill for us when we get to see the new baby of one of our patients. Finally, we meet our small ultrasound patient in living color!

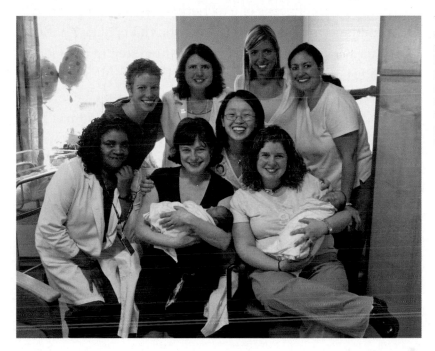

When Lydia delivered her twins, the ultrasound staff had to visit her in her hospital room and get a picture of everyone holding the babies! (The proud mother is in the middle.)

Labor Begins: Opening the Gateway to Birth

Birth happens in many different ways. Some are planned as vaginal deliveries and progress as expected. Some are planned cesarean sections (c-sections) if that is deemed the safest choice. Some are planned as vaginal births, but in the end become c-section births if it is decided that is best for the mother and baby. Here we'll discuss what happens in a typical vaginal birth, but of course there are many differences you may experience, small and large, just as there are many different mothers and babies.

For many women who deliver vaginally, the first clue that labor is beginning is regularly spaced contractions, which feel like the uterus is tightening and then relaxing. Some women might first notice mucous or experience a rush of water when the membranes rupture and the amniotic fluid pours out. But no matter what the signals may be, the final step in the journey of pregnancy has begun, and now the powerful momentum of nature cannot be denied. At this point, it is time to call the doctor or midwife and collect that small suitcase that may have been packed and ready for weeks.

Once the woman enters the delivery room, she and her support person (or people, on occasion) are usually excited and nervous, especially as doctors or other caregivers begin to examine the pregnant woman and assess the baby's well-being. What are they looking for? And what are they talking about? What do *"effacement"* and *"dilation"* mean, anyway? In the following section, we—with the help of Lydia and her experience as obstetrician and mother—will tell you. We begin with a look at what is going on inside the woman's body during labor.

The Transforming Cervix

Labor begins when the uterus contracts regularly, causing the cervix to open (*dilate*). The labor pains an expectant mother feels are due to these contractions—they are opening the way for the baby to emerge. For a woman undergoing a vaginal birth, much of the action during labor and delivery is centered in the cervix. It is the gateway between the body of the uterus and the vagina, the baby's passageway into the world. It is a cylinder-shaped muscular organ—usually between one and a quarter and two inches in length—with a canal down the middle. For almost all of a woman's life, that canal remains closed except for a thin opening through which sperm can enter during intercourse and through which blood can exit during menstrual periods.

For most of pregnancy the cervical canal is closed, keeping the baby inside the uterus. During the first stage of labor, the contractions of the uterus cause the cervix to gradually open as well as shorten and thin out (*efface*). This sequence is illustrated in the diagram below, which shows what the cervix looks like during pregnancy.

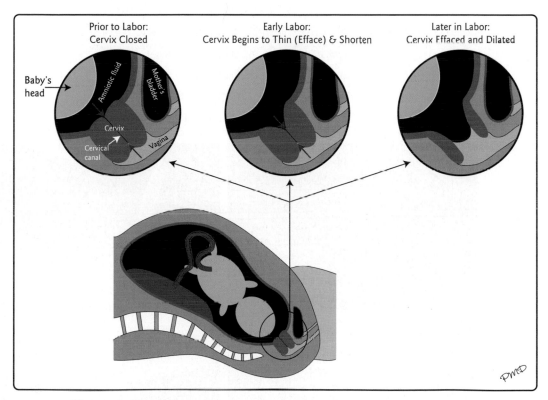

The cervix during pregnancy

The cervix is thick, long, and closed for most of pregnancy, then changes dramatically during labor.

The top left part of the diagram on page 169 shows what the cervix looks like before labor. The closed cervical canal extends from its inner end on the baby's side of the cervix (the *internal os*) to the outer end touching the vagina (the *external os*). The opening starts at the internal os, as shown in the top middle part of the diagram, while the rest of the cervix remains closed. At this point the cervix is partially effaced, as the inner portion is thinner and the length of the cervical canal (between the arrowheads) is shorter than it was before labor.

The Fully Dilated Cervix: Ready for Birth

The widening and thinning of the cervix progresses until the cervix is open along its entire length, as shown in the top right of the diagram on page 169. The first stage of labor is completed when the cervix is fully effaced and ten centimeters (four inches) dilated. If this doesn't happen or takes a very long time to happen, a c-section may be considered.

The cervix on a quiet day

A 2D ultrasound shows what a normal cervix looks like during most of the pregnancy, with the central canal closed. The calipers and arrowheads show how the cervix is measured; the length of the cervix is nearly two inches, which is normal.

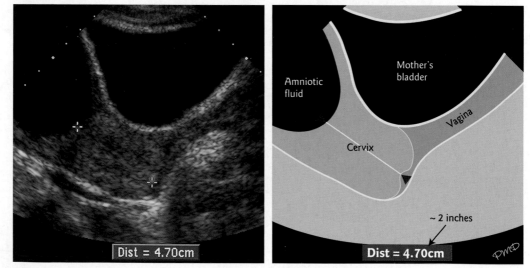

170

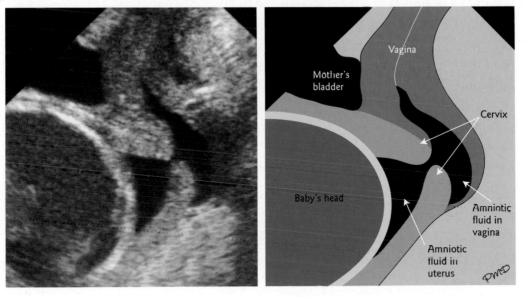

Head first!

The cervix is fully effaced but only partially dilated, still not at the ten centimeters needed to begin pushing. The membranes have ruptured, so fluid is present within the vagina as well as the uterus. The baby's head is poised and ready to come out through the vagina.

For another way to view the cervix before and during labor, look at the ultrasound images and diagrams on the preceding page and above. The first two illustrations show the cervix before labor, and the second two show it partially dilated and completely effaced, with the baby's head poised to exit through it.

Labor Continues: Pushing the Baby Out

Once the cervix is fully effaced and ten centimeters dilated, the second stage of labor begins. Now, the very-soon-to-be new mother is ready to start pushing the baby out into the world. At this point, the chorionic and amniotic membranes may already have ruptured—the "water breaking—or the membranes may bulge into the dilated cervix and will rupture shortly.

As Lydia explains, the momentum usually begins to build quickly in the delivery room: "Once the cervix is fully dilated, the baby's head can descend through the vagina. At that point, mom can start pushing hard, and we all—doctors, nurses, the labor coach—usually start counting with every push. Some mothers will reach their hand down to feel the crowning of the baby's head; others will ask for a mirror to watch the peeking of their baby's head with each push. To encourage her, we might talk about how much hair there is on the baby's head, or what color it is."

The hard work of labor is a powerful experience for most mothers. Lydia tells us, "With each push, she can feel the descent of her baby and know that it is the result of all her efforts and the good care she has taken of her body. It is amazingly satisfying: her strength is bringing this baby into the world."

As the mother and her support person continue to count with each push, they are both also aware that the climactic moment of birth is coming closer and closer. In Lydia's experience, "In those last few minutes, all of the emotional energy of every person in the delivery room is channeling into that birth canal!"

Welcome to the World!

When the baby's head emerges, the shoulders, then arms and legs, usually follow quickly, and within five minutes, the baby is born and announced (a healthy boy or girl—or sometimes more). "We all hold our breath as the baby takes his own first breath and utters his first cry," Lydia relates. "This is when parents usually start to cry as well. No matter if it is their first baby or their sixth, it is always an overwhelming, amazing moment. We are hearing the voice of a new person who was

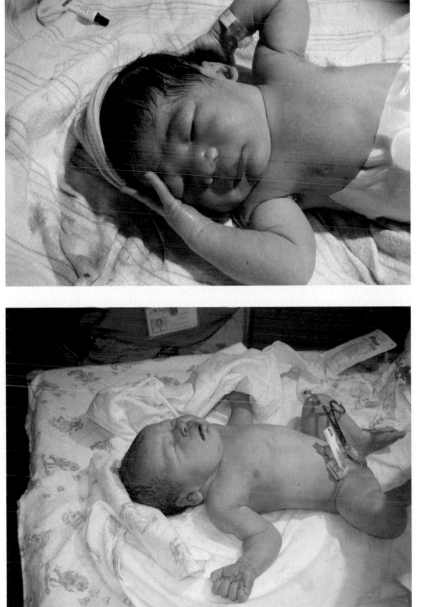

A brand-new
baby boy

A baby girl, taking
her first breaths

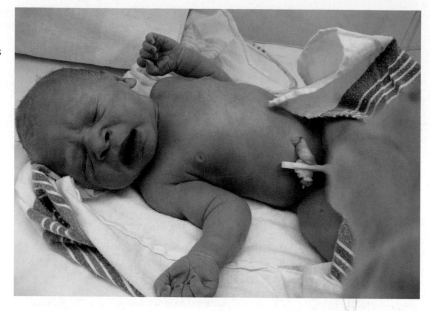

A newborn boy, born by c-section. His doctor cheered, "Happy Birthday!" as he emerged into the world and was brought to his mother.

not in the room five minutes ago, and we all experience a profound sense of hope at the possibilities of this new life."

These emotions are the same whether baby has entered the world through vaginal birth or c-section. Even though c-section is a surgery, the mother is almost always awake with her partner or coach by her side, joining doctors, nurses, and other medical experts cheering the baby's entry into the world.

Once the baby has come out of the mother's body and can breathe on her own, the umbilical cord has served its purpose. Lydia explains, "We clamp the umbilical cord and ask if the partner would like to cut it. Then we put the baby immediately on mom's chest, skin to skin. This reassures the baby and keeps her warm." At this point, the baby is still wet and covered with the white coating called *vernix*.

"We wipe the baby off, and some mothers might begin to nurse right away," said Lydia. "Birth is a universal experience— yet no one remembers one's own birth. It is an experience that

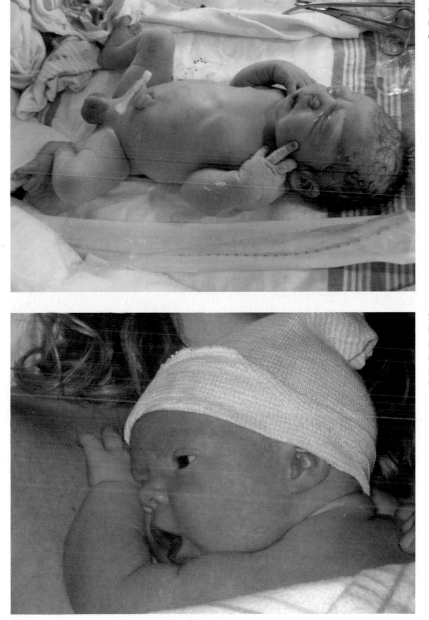

A baby boy, moments after his umbilical cord was clamped and cut

Seconds after the birth, the baby is usually given to the new mother—an incredible moment for all involved.

can only be witnessed and remembered by others. As a mother and obstetrician, I feel reborn with each birth that I have experienced or assisted. I relive the miracle of life every day at work!"

A father cherishes his newborn baby

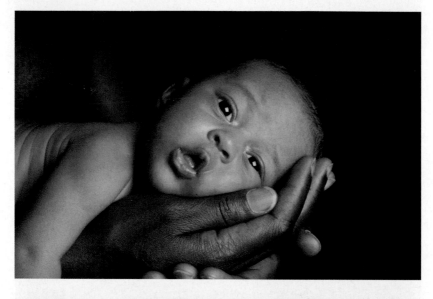

A mother and daughter enjoying their first moments together

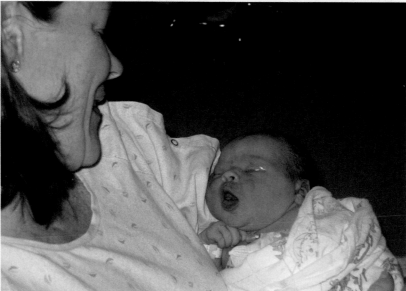

Getting Personal

As we mentioned earlier in this book, in addition to being physicians and a married couple, we are also parents. Between us, we have five children, now grown. But—like all parents—we hold every one of our birth and newborn experiences indelibly in our memories. We share some early childhood pictures with you here.

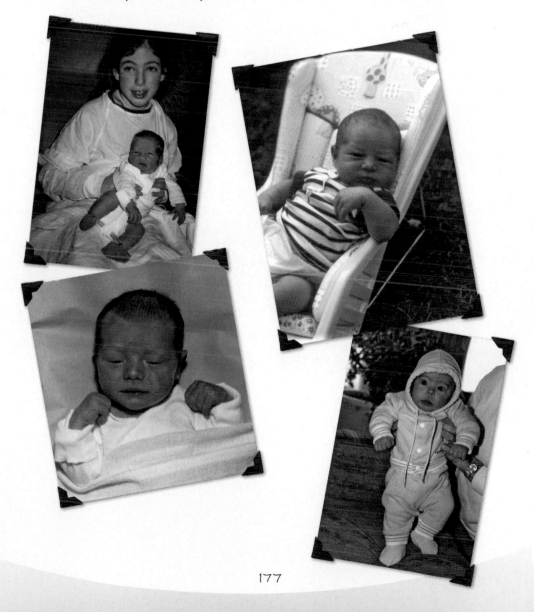

My Baby's Ultrasound Printouts

More About Ultrasound

An ultrasound procedure (*sonogram* or *scan*) is performed through the expectant mother's abdomen (*transabdominal* ultrasound) or vagina (*transvaginal* ultrasound). Transabdominal ultrasound is painless, and transvaginal ultrasound should involve at most minimal discomfort. Both are fascinating for the parents-to-be, who can watch the moving images of their baby on the screen. The mother lies on her back and the *sonographer* (technologist trained in ultrasound) or doctor moves a *transducer* coated in gel around on her abdomen or in her vagina. The transducer both looks and functions like a large two-way microphone: it transmits inaudible, high-frequency sound waves into the body and then "listens" for the echoes that come back as the sound waves bounce off internal structures of mother and baby. A computer in the ultrasound machine then translates these reflected sound waves into images that you can see on a screen.

So, to sum up, an ultrasound machine consists of a microphone attached to a computer, which converts sound waves into images that appear on a screen. The images can be of various types, and a single sonogram often produces more than one type of image, as seen in the figure on the next page. The types include the following.

2D Ultrasound 3D Ultrasound Color Doppler Ultrasound Spectral Doppler Ultrasound

Ultrasound: how it is done and what forms it takes

Two-Dimensional (2D) Ultrasound

Two-dimensional refers to a flat surface, so 2D ultrasound produces images that are like slices through the body. This is the most commonly used form of ultrasound because it is best suited to examining the baby's internal organs to make sure development is normal.

A good way to think of 2D ultrasound is by imagining a loaf of bread. When you slice a piece, you can look at the flat surface of the slice (a two-dimensional object) and see the texture of the dough, as well as the location and size of any air pockets, nuts, or raisins.

In a similar way, when the transducer is placed on the mother's abdomen, it sends back information that is translated into an image "slice." The sound waves pass through her skin, her abdominal muscles, the wall of the uterus, the amniotic fluid surrounding the baby, the baby's skin, and into the baby's internal organs—such as the heart or the brain. The information sent back to the computer creates a two-dimensional slice of all of those tissues and structures, allowing the doctor to examine the baby's organs closely. (CT scans use similar imaging techniques.)

The beauty of ultrasound is that, unlike slicing a loaf of bread, you can see all of these internal structures without actually cutting a slice of the mother! The sound waves and their returning echoes pass painlessly through skin, organs, and other tissues. The first picture at the top of the illustration on page 180 shows a 2D ultrasound image of a (purely visual!) "slice" of a baby's brain, as if you were looking down on it after the top of the head has been "removed." If the doctor wants to see a different organ, or the same organ from a different perspective, the transducer can be angled, moved to a different spot on the abdomen, or rotated. This is why ultrasound images may show slices of different body parts that are horizontal, vertical, or in profile. The images on the screen are also refreshed approximately thirty times a second, so you can see the baby actually moving in real time on video.

Three-Dimensional (3D) Ultrasound

By adding the third dimension—depth—to an ultrasound image, we use exactly the same sound wave energy, but the computer displays the returning echoes in a different way. Three-dimensional (3D) ultrasound is often used to show the outer surface of the baby and produces images that are most recognizable to the parents. It may supplement the 2D imaging to make sure the baby is developing normally.

Three-dimensional ultrasound technology allows you to see the baby as if you were actually inside the uterus looking at the baby as it floats in the amniotic fluid. When used in this way, 3D ultrasound ignores everything between the surface of the mother's abdomen and the baby itself. Unlike 2D ultrasound, however, you would not see the baby's internal organs. The second picture in the illustration shows the strikingly recognizable image of a baby's face as seen with 3D ultrasound.

When the baby is very small, early in the pregnancy, the 3D image might show the entire body. But as it grows larger, the image reveals only limited areas of the body, and the doctor or sonographer will move or angle the transducer to show different parts or perspectives. Like 2D ultrasound, 3D ultrasound can also capture the baby's movement.

Color Doppler Ultrasound

The nineteenth-century Austrian mathematician Christian Andreas Doppler (1803–1853) was the first to describe the *Doppler effect*, a phenomenon by which motion affects the frequency—or pitch—of sound waves. If you stand next to a railroad track and a train rushes by, the sound of the train whistle is higher pitched as it approaches you and lower in pitch as it moves away from you. This is the Doppler effect. Similarly, as blood flows through arteries and veins in the body, the movement of the blood cells changes the pitch (frequency) of the sound waves echoing back to the ultrasound transducer. These changes in pitch allow us to measure the amount and rate of blood flowing in arteries and veins. For example, in the third illustration the color Doppler image is combined with a two-dimensional image of the head to show blood flowing through major arteries in the brain. Images like this one allow the doctor to look at important blood vessels in the developing baby.

Spectral Doppler Ultrasound

Instead of showing the flow of blood by color on the ultrasound image, as with color Doppler, spectral Doppler ultrasound produces a graph that shows the velocity (speed) of blood flow in an artery or vein as it varies over time. Like other forms of ultrasound, this can be used to create images from within the bodies of both baby and mother. The last picture in our illustration shows a spectral Doppler image of blood flowing between the placenta and baby through the umbilical cord. The screen is split: the top half shows a 2D image of the umbilical cord, and the bottom half shows the speed of blood flow over time. The peaks along the graph occur when the baby's heart contracts, squeezing out a burst of blood at a high rate of speed. When the baby's heart relaxes between contractions, and the flow of blood becomes slower, the height of the Doppler curve goes down. The spectral Doppler image can be used to evaluate blood flow through any artery or vein.

Index

A

Abdomen, 61
  growth of, 100f
  measurement of, 94, 96, 99
  organs in, 66–70
Age
  conceptual, 6
  gestational (*See* Gestational age)
  of mother, 137
American Institute of Ultrasound
    in Medicine, xi
Amniocentesis, 137, 138–40
  chorionic villus sampling
      compared with, 140–41
  images of, 139f, 140f
  purpose of, 138
  safety of, 138
  Tay-Sachs diagnosed with,
      159–60
Amnion, 38, 134
  function of, 6
  images of, 38f
  of twins, 109, 110, 111, 112
Amniotic fluid, 6, 38, 43, 70, 125,
    127, 133–35, 168
  amount of, 134–35
  dynamics of, 134
  functions of, 133
  images of, 38f, 135f
  low levels of, 158
  in the lungs, 63–64
  swallowing of, 51, 68, 134
  urination and, 92, 134

Amniotic membrane, 171
Anemia, 144, 160–61
Aorta, 65–66, 154f
Arms, 11, 39
  development of, 77–80
  images of, 78f, 80f
Arteries
  of the brain, 55
  iliac, 70
  pulmonary, 66, 154f
  renal, 70
  umbilical, 70, 127, 132, 158
Atria, 14, 64, 65, 66
Autonomic nervous system, 63

B

Belly button, 6, 46, 75, 129
Benson, Carol B. (background),
    x–xii
Birth, 165–77. *See also* Delivery;
    Labor
Bladder, 66, 69–70
Blastocyst, 31
Blood
  circulation system, 45
  separation of mother-baby, 6
Blood flow, 132–33, 158, 160,
    183–84
Blood transfusions, 144,
    160–61
Body, 36, 61–75. *See also*
    Abdomen; Chest; Spine

Bones
  of arms and hands, 79–80
  development of, 44
  of legs and feet, 80–81
  of ribs, 61
  of skull, 44, 53
  of spine, 73–74
Boys, sexual organs of, 87–89
Brain, 53, 54–59, 68, 71, 72
  hemispheres of, 54, 56
  images of, 4f, 10f, 53f, 54f, 55f,
    57f, 59f
  mother's, 17, 20
  plumbing system of, 55
  rapid growth of, 56
  relationship to support
    structures, 56
  structures of, 54–55
  surface of, 58, 59f
Breastbone. *See* Sternum
Breathing, 62, 63–64, 172
Brigham and Women's Hospital, x

Carbon dioxide, 127, 130
Cartilage, 44
  of arms, 78, 80
  of legs, 78
  of ribs, 61
  of spine, 73–74
Cerebellum
  functions of, 54–55
  images of, 54f
  measurement of, 102
Cerebrospinal fluid, 55, 71, 75
Cerebrum, 54

Cervical canal, 22, 169, 170
Cervical spine, 72, 74, 75
Cervix, 22
  dilation of, 168, 170–71
  effacement of, 168, 169–70,
    171
  images of, 23f, 169f, 170f,
    171f
  size and shape of, 168–69
  transformation during labor,
    168–71
Cesarean section (c-section), 94,
    128, 158, 166, 170, 174
Chest, 53, 61, 62–66
Chorion, 38, 127, 134, 141
  function of, 6
  of twins, 109, 110, 111, 112
Chorionic fluid, 134
Chorionic membrane, 127, 171
Chorionic villi, 141, 142
Chorionic villus sampling
    (CVS), 137, 140–43
  images of, 141f, 142f, 143f
  indications for, 140–41
  transabdominal, 142–43
  transcervical, 142–43
Choroid plexus, 55, 56
Chromosomes
  sex, 87, 90
  total number of, 30
Circulation systems, 45–46
Colon, 69
Color Doppler ultrasound, 70, 92
  description of procedure, 183
  example of imagery, 180f
Conceptual age, 6
Contractions, 168, 169
Corpus luteum, 21, 31

Crown-rump length, 36, 94

CVS. *See* Chorionic villus
    sampling

D

Decidua, 31, 127, 142

Delivery, 171–72. *See also*
    Cesarean section; Vaginal
    delivery

Diaphragm, 63–64

Dichorionic-diamniotic (di-di)
    twins, 109, 110f

Differentiation, 31

Diffusion, 134

Digestive system, 68

Dilation of cervix, 168, 170–71

Dionne quintuplets, 119, 120

Discs (spinal), 71

Dizygotic twins. *See* Fraternal
    (dizygotic) twins

Dominant follicle, 20, 21, 149

Doppler, Christian Andreas, 183

Doppler effect, 183

Doppler gate, 132

Doubilet, Peter M. (background),
    x–xii

Down syndrome, 138

Dreaming, 83

Due date, assigning of, 6

E

Ectopic pregnancy, 151–52

Effacement of cervix, 168, 169–70,
    171

Eggs, 17, 22, 24, 109
    fertility drugs and, 21, 119–20
    monthly production schedule,
        18–21
    number of chromosomes in,
        30

Embryo, 6
    freezing of, 149–50
    images of, 7f

Endometrium, 19, 22–24
    function of, 24
    images of, 23f
    transformation of, 30–31

Endoscopic camera, viii

Epiphysis, 78

Esophagus, 68

Estrogen, 18, 19, 24

External os, 170

Extremities, 77. *See also* Arms;
    Legs

Eyes, 4f, 45f, 53

F

Face, 10, 53
    images of, 10f, 52f
    mood changes glimpsed on,
        51

Fallopian tubes, 22, 24, 109
    blocked, 148
    images of, 23f
    peristalsis in, 30
    structure and function of,
        20–21

Falx, 54

Feet, 12, 78, 80–81

Femur, 81, 94, 96, 101

Fertility treatment
    case study of, 148–51
    multiple pregnancies and, 21,
        119–20, 150–51
Fertilization, 5, 24–25, 29, 30
    reactions following, 21
    twinning and, 108, 109, 111
Fetal position, 42
Fetus, 6
Fingers, 11, 80
First trimester
    amniotic fluid expansion in,
        134–35
    bone development during, 44
    from cells to structure during,
        31–36
    early, 29–39
    late, 41–47
    length of, 6
    measurement in, 94
    microscopic biological
        explosion during, 30–31
    overview, 7–9
    protection and nourishment
        during, 36–39
    rapid growth during, 29, 31–32,
        34–36, 41, 43
Follicles, 18–20, 31, 149
    dominant, 20, 21, 149
    images of, 20f, 149f
Fontanel, 44
Fraternal (dizygotic) twins, 108,
    109, 116, 150–51
    genetic makeup of, 107
    images of, 108f, 115f, 150f
    ultrasound identification of, 112
Fundus, 22, 23f

Gallbladder, 66, 69
Genetics
    of fraternal twins, 107
    of identical twins, 108
    measurement information on,
        95
    tests for disorders (See
        Amniocentesis; Chorionic
        villus sampling)
Genital ducts, 87
Gestational age, ix
    defined, 6, 29
    determination by
        measurement, 94, 96
Gestational sac, 5, 31, 32, 33, 42,
    109, 127, 134, 135
    amniocentesis and, 138
    during chorionic villus
        sampling, 142, 143
    images of, 5f, 32f, 33f, 34f
    structure and function of, 6
Girls, sexual organs of, 90–91
Growth plate, 78–79, 80
Gyri, 58

Hands, 11, 78, 79–80
Harvard Medical School, x
Head, 53. See also Brain
    first appearance of, 39
    growth of, 98f
    images of, 8f, 10f, 37f
    measurement of, 94, 96, 97

Health
    measurements as indicator of, 94–95
    movement as indicator of, 83–85
    preventing problems in, 147–61
    tests for, 137–46
Heart, 61, 62
    diagnosing problems of, 153–54
    first appearance of, 14, 29
    images of, 14f, 65f, 154f
    structures of, 64–66
Heartbeat, 7, 29, 33, 132–33
Hormones, 17, 18, 20, 21, 24
Human chorionic gonadotropin (hCG), 21
Humerus, 79, 80f, 102

Identical (monozygotic) twins, 107, 112–14, 116
    dichorionic-diamniotic, 109
    genetic makeup of, 108
    images of, 108f, 113f, 114f
    monochorionic-diamniotic, 110
    monochorionic-monoamniotic, 111
    ultrasound identification of, 112
Iliac arteries, 70
Implantation, 31
In vitro fertilization (IVF), 120, 148–51

Internal os, 170
Intestines, 66, 68–69
Intrauterine insemination, 120

Kidneys, 66
    diagnosing problems of, 154–56
    images of, 69f, 155f
    structure and functions of, 69–70

Labia, 90
Labor, 167–72
    beginning of, 167–71
    premature, 94
    pushing baby out, 171–72
Last menstrual period (LMP), 6, 94
Lee, Lydia K., 166–67, 168, 171–76
Legs, 12, 35–36, 39, 77–79
    development of, 80–81
    images of, 81f, 82f
Ligaments, 71
Lips, 53
Liver, 66, 69
Lumbar spine, 72–73, 74, 75
Lungs, 61, 65, 66
    amniocentesis testing of, 138
    images of, 64f, 65f
    structure and development of, 62–64
Lymphatic system, 45–46

Measurement, 81, 94–103
    reasons for, 94–95
    routine, 95–96
Menstrual cycle, 18–21, 22,
    24–25
Menstrual period, 18–19, 21, 25,
    169. *See also* Last menstrual
    period
Mitral valve, 65
Monochorionic-diamniotic
    (mono-di) twins, 110
Monochorionic-monoamniotic
    (mono-mono) twins, 111
Monozygotic twins. *See*
    Identical (monozygotic)
    twins
Mouth, 4f, 10, 68
Movement, ix, 77, 82–85
    brain structures responsible for,
        54–55
    health and, 83–85
    images of, 83f, 84f, 85f
    mother's sensation of, 82
Multiple pregnancies, ix,
    107–17.
        See also Twins
    fertility drugs and, 21, 119–20,
        150–51
    fraternal and identical
        groupings in, 120
    higher-order, 119–22
    images of, 120f, 121f,
        122f
Myometrium, 22, 23f

Nasal bone, 102, 103f
Nose, 4f, 45f, 53
Nourishment/nutrition, 36–39,
    127–28
    insufficient, 95, 157–59
    pathway to, 46–47
Nuchal fold, 102
Nuchal translucency, 46, 94,
    102

Oocytes, 18
Os, internal and external,
    170
Ossification, 44, 73, 78,
    80
Ovaries, 5, 17
    development of, 90
    images of, 19f
    role of in pregnancy,
        18–21
Ovulation, 20, 24, 30
Oxygen supply, 62, 65, 66, 70,
    127, 130, 157

Pelvis, 61, 62f
Penis, 87–88, 89f
Peristalsis, 30
Pituitary gland, 17

Placenta, 33, 46, 47, 62, 65, 66,
 125, 127–28, 134
  blood delivery to, 70, 127
  blood vessels of, 126
  chorionic villus sampling and,
   141, 142–43
  development of, 31, 38
  images of, 38f, 126f, 128f, 131f,
   146f
  insufficient nourishment from,
   95, 157–59
  location of, 128, 142–43, 144–46
  structure and function of, 6, 127
  of twins, 109, 110, 111
  umbilical blood sampling and,
   144–46
  umbilical cord connection to,
   6, 31, 130, 131f, 144–45
Placenta previa, 128, 129f
Pregnancy, 3–15. *See also* First
   trimester; Multiple
   pregnancies; Second
   trimester; Third trimester
  the body's preparation for, 5, 17–25
  ectopic, 151–52
  terms used in, 6
Premature labor, 94
Progesterone, 18, 21, 24
Proliferative phase of menstrual
   cycle, 24
Protection
  for the developing baby, 36–39,
   133
  of the spinal cord, 75
  thoracic spine and, 72
Pulmonary artery, 66, 154f

Quadruplets, 120, 122f
Quickening, 77
Quintuplets, 119, 120

Radius, 79, 80f
Rapid-eye-movement (REM)
   sleep, 53, 83
Reflux, 156
Renal arteries, 70
Rh antibodies, 160–61
Ribs, 13, 61, 62f, 72, 74

S/D ratio, 133
Sacral spine, 72, 73, 74
Safety
  of amniocentesis, 138
  of ultrasound, xi
Scrotum, 88, 89f, 90
Second trimester. *See also*
   Arms; Body; Face; Head;
   Legs; Movement; Sexual
   organs
  amniotic fluid during, 134, 135
  length of, 6
  measurement in, 94, 95, 97
  overview, 10–15
Secretory phase of menstrual
   cycle, 24

Sexual organs, 87–92
  of boys, 87–89
  of girls, 90–91
  images of, 88f, 89f, 90f, 91f, 92f
Shaft (bone), 78, 79–80, 81
Size, of baby, 93–95, 157–59. *See also* Measurement
Skull bones, 44, 53
Sleep, 53, 82–83
Sonograms, viii, x, 179
Sonographer, 154–55, 179
Sonography. *See* Ultrasound imaging/scanning
Spectral Doppler ultrasound, 132–33
  description of procedure, 183–84
  example of imagery, 180f
Sperm, 21, 30, 169
Spinal canal, 71, 75
Spinal cord
  protection of, 75
  structure and functions of, 71–72
Spine, 13, 61, 71–75
  bone formation in, 73–74
  cervical, 72, 74, 75
  images of, 12f, 13f, 62f, 73f, 74f, 75f
  lumbar, 72–73, 74, 75
  sacral, 72, 73, 74
  structure and functions of, 71–73
  thoracic, 72, 73, 74, 75
Sternum, 61, 64, 72
Stomach, 66, 68–69
Subarachnoid space, 55

Sulci, 58
Swallowing, 10, 51, 68, 134

Tay-Sachs disease, 159–60
Temperature control, 133
Testicles, 88, 89f, 90
Testosterone, 87, 90
Tests, diagnostic, 137–46
Third trimester. *See also* Arms; Body; Face; Head; Legs; Movement; Sexual organs
  amniotic fluid during, 134
  length of, 6
  measurement in, 94, 95, 96, 97
  overview, 10–15
Thoracic spine, 72, 73, 74, 75
Three-dimensional (3D) ultrasound, vii, ix, 8
  description of procedure, 182
  example of imagery, 180f
  power of imagery, 51
  type of image produced by, viii
Thumb, 80
Thumb sucking, 10, 51, 84
Trachea, 63
Transabdominal chorionic villus sampling (CVS), 142–43
Transabdominal ultrasound, 179
Transcervical chorionic villus sampling (CVS), 142–43
Transducer, 179, 181–82
Transvaginal ultrasound, 32, 179
Tricuspid valve, 65

Trimesters, 6. *See also* First trimester; Second trimester; Third trimester
Triplets, 21, 119, 120, 121f, 122f
Trunk, 61, 62f
Twins, 21, 107–17, 166. *See also* Fraternal (dizygotic) twins; Identical (monozygotic) twins
  dichorionic-diamniotic, 109, 110f
  images of, 108f, 110f, 113f, 114f, 115f, 116f, 117f, 150f
  incidence of, 107
  monochorionic-diamniotic, 110
  monochorionic-monoamniotic, 111
Two-dimensional (2D) ultrasound, 8
  applications of, ix–x
  brain images on, 53
  description of procedure, 181–82
  example of imagery, 180f
  heart images on, 14
  type of image produced by, viii

U

Ulna, 79, 80f
Ultrasound imaging/scanning, vii–x, 179–84. *See also* Color Doppler ultrasound; Spectral Doppler ultrasound; Three-dimensional (3D) ultrasound; Two-dimensional (2D) ultrasound
  accuracy of measurements, 94
  amniocentesis guidance with, 138–40, 159
  applications of, ix–x
  bone on, 44
  chorionic villus sampling guidance with, 142, 143
  description of equipment, 179
  description of technique, vii–viii
  diagnostic uses of, 147–61
  early movement shown on, 82
  examples of imagery types, 180f
  first images on, 29, 30, 32, 33
  safety of, xi
  transabdominal, 179
  transvaginal, 32, 179
  as twin detective, 112
  umbilical blood sampling guidance with, 144, 145, 160, 161
  video, vii, ix, 182
Umbilical arteries, 70, 127, 132, 158
Umbilical blood sampling, 137, 144–46, 160
Umbilical cord, 6, 31, 38, 44, 65, 125, 134
  blood delivery to, 70
  cutting of, 15, 174
  function of, 15, 46–47, 66, 126–27, 129–33
  images of, 9f, 11f, 12f, 15f, 39f, 45f, 47f, 67f, 70f, 130f, 131f, 132f, 133f
  size of, 129

Umbilical cord, *continued*
    structure of, 129–33
    of twins, 111
Umbilical vein, 127, 132, 144,
      145, 161
Ureters, 69–70, 156
Urethra, 70
Urine/urination, 69–70, 92, 134.
    See also Waste elimination
Uterine body, 22, 23f
Uterine cavity, 22, 23f, 24
Uterus, 5, 20, 21–25, 30
    changes in, 21–22
    environment of, 24–25
    images of, 23f
    potential space of, 22–24
    structure and functions of, 22

Vagina, 90
Vaginal delivery, 167–72, 174
Vein, umbilical, 127, 132, 144,
      145, 161
Ventricles (brain), 55, 56
Ventricles (heart), 14, 64, 65f, 66
Vernix, 174
Vertebrae, 13
    function of, 71
    images of, 13f
    types of, 72–73

Vertebral body, 71
Video ultrasounds, vii, ix, 182

Waste elimination, 69, 126f,
    127, 130. *See also*
    Urine/urination
Water, breaking of, 133, 168,
    171
Weight, estimation of, 94–95,
    96
Wharton's jelly, 129

X chromosomes, 87, 90

Y chromosome, 87
Yolk sac, 32, 46–47
    disappearance of, 47
    function of, 33
    images of, 33f, 34f, 37f, 47f

Zygote, 30–31, 107, 108